Something Rich and Strange:

Discovering Your Path
to Wholeness

Susan Davis, Ph.D.

WESTBOW
PRESS
A DIVISION OF THOMAS NELSON

Unless otherwise noted, all scripture is taken from THE MESSAGE. Copyright ©1993, 1994, 1995, 1996, 2000, 2001, 2002. sed by permission of NavPress Publishing Group.

Grateful acknowledgment is made for permission to reprint the following copyrighted works:

Cummings, E. E., "a total stranger one black day". Copyright ©1957, 1985, 1991 by the Trustees for the E. E. Cummings Trust, from SELECTED POEMS by E. E. Cummings, Introduction & Commentary Richard S. Kennedy. Used by permission of Liveright Publishing Corporation.

Hopkins, Gerard Manley: "Pied Beauty" and "Carrion Comfort". Copyright ©1970 from THE POEMS OF GERARD MANLEY HOPKINS 4e, edited by W.H. Gardener and N.H. MacKenzie. Used by permission of Oxford University Press on behalf of the British Province of the Society of Jesus.

Hughes, Langston: "Mother to Son" from THE COLLECTED POEMS OF LANGSTON HUGHES by Langston Hughes, edited by Arnold Rampersad with David Roessel, Associate Editor, copyright ©1994 by the Estate of Langston Hughes. Used by permission of Alfred A. Knopf, a division of Random House, Inc. Electronic versions used by permission of Harold Ober Associates Incorporated. Copyright ©1994.

Cover graphics by Ruby Mosquera
Imagery inspired by the reflections of a client:
    "When you are in the forest at night, you can't see where you are going, it's so dark--but if you look up, you can see the path."

WestBow Press books may be ordered through booksellers or by contacting:

WestBow Press
A Division of Thomas Nelson
1663 Liberty Drive
Bloomington, IN 47403
www.westbowpress.com
1-(866) 928-1240

ISBN: 978-1-4497-2821-2 (sc)
ISBN: 978-1-4497-2890-8 (e)
Library of Congress Control Number: 2011918043

Printed in the United States of America
WestBow Press rev. date: 11/18/2011

I come from a line of gutsy and going on women[1]—

for my grandmother, my mother, and my sisters—
and for my daughters:
Meagan, Kristen, and Hanna.

---

[1] This phrase is adapted from Lucille Clifton's poem *for deLawd*, published in her book, *Good Woman: Poems and a Memoir 1969-1980*, (Rochester, New York: BOA Editions, Ltd., 1987), p. 32.

Contents

Foreword by Eugene Peterson

"The great irony in America today is that we know so much and can do so much and that we live so badly." These words are from Walker Percy. He wrote five penetrating novels exploring this irony, just in case we hadn't noticed.

More recently, Tony Judt, out of a lifetime of exquisite political writing, titled his final book *Ill Fares the Land* published shortly before his premature death in 2010. The title is a line lifted from Oliver Goldsmith's 1770 poem "The Deserted Village,"

> *Ill fares the land, to hastening ills a prey;*
> *Where wealth accumulates, and men decay.*

We are fortunate to have voices like Percy and Judt giving careful attention to how badly we are living and that, despite (or maybe because of) our high standard of living, the pain, suffering, and discontent abroad in the land continues to accumulate.

One conspicuous response to what is wrong with the world these days seems to be anger, not infrequently expressed in hate, blaming randomly selected scapegoats. It seems to many of us a cheap way to use these precious lives of ours, bodies and souls that are capable of nurturing beauty and loving our neighbors.

The good news is that there is also a quite incredible company of men and women, far outnumbering the naysayers, who devote their lives to alleviating the pain, mitigating the suffering, dealing with the discontent, and protecting the weak and vulnerable: writers and pastors, healers and counselors, social workers and teachers, advocates for the poor and disadvantaged, artists and farmers, parents and grandparents, police and firefighters, volunteers and philanthropists.

For the most part these people do their work quietly, often unnoticed and unremarked, directing their energies, skills, and compassion to helping and guiding others to live good, wholesome and healthy lives.

Susan Davis, a psychotherapist, is one of these. This book is an invitation to participate in a relationship with her by reading and appreciating who she is and what she is doing.

What is striking and attractive to me is her skill in integrating so much that is involved in the healing of emotions and childhood abuse, work relationships, and intimacies into a whole and good life, a journey of transformation. She tells the stories of her clients, but never by reducing them to problems to be fixed. There is nothing impersonal or condescending in her work. The stories provide the living context for her work. But there is more; she is in touch and familiar with poets and other writers who deal wisely and skillfully with the subtlety and ambiguity of so much of what is involved in being a human being on this planet earth. In the process we realize that she is an excellent teacher, familiar with and adept at employing the psychological insights of accomplished men and women that give clarity to the hidden or suppressed parts of life.

The most distinctive thing about Dr. Davis' account of her work is that in weaving this tapestry using the threads of story, poetry, and psychology, she does her work on a loom constructed from the parallel stories of the exodus of the Hebrews from twelfth century Egypt and the death and resurrection of Jesus in first century Jerusalem, citing a text from Luke ("they talked over his exodus, the one Jesus was about to complete in Jerusalem"). This large, all-encompassing "loom" of biblical story, Exodus and Jesus, holding all the threads in a tight weave, provides an always available orientation for understanding and achieving a life of transformation that enters into and embraces a life in continuity with our fathers and mothers who have been on speaking terms with God and his ways, continuously documented now for three thousand years.

The practice of contemporary psychotherapy set here in the immense context of the Hebrew exodus and Jesus' resurrection stories prevents psychotherapy from being reductionist, flattened into a secularized individualism. At the same time it prevents us from warehousing the Scripture accounts of transformation as archives of interest only to research scholars.

Reading *Something Rich and Strange* puts us in the unhurried and gentle company of a friend. As we find ourselves treated with dignity and God treated with reverence, on the transformation journey, we realize we are in good company, very good company indeed—we don't have to "live so badly."

Eugene H. Peterson
Professor Emeritus of Spiritual Theology
Regent College, Vancouver, B.C.

Nothing of him that doth fade
But doth suffer a sea-change
Into something rich and strange.
William Shakespeare

Preface

Understanding the process of transformation—how we suffer a sea-change, as Shakespeare said—and the result of that becoming—something rich and strange[2]—is the reason for this book. It is the hero's journey, the adventure of becoming fully ourselves and fully alive.

Becoming "fully ourselves and fully alive" sounds great, but though we may long for a change in our lives or ourselves, we humans usually resist it. We prefer the familiar and safe, even when it is costly or painful. So often we are pushed down the path to wholeness, our comfort disturbed. Yet, whether the journey of transformation is thrust upon us or sought out, it will be awe-full and wonder-filled. It takes place where the spiritual and the psychological overlap, in the depths of the psyche. Like the birth process that occurs without our conscious control, it surprises us and unfolds with a power and a wisdom of its own. Also like the human birth process, we can facilitate and enhance the transformative process—whether our own

---

[2] William Shakespeare, *The Tempest*. Act I. Sc. 2.

or someone else's—by understanding it and choosing courageously to embrace it.

At times on the journey we may feel afraid and alone, but the path is well traveled, as we will see. "It is, I think, that we are all so alone in what lies deepest in our souls, so unable to find the words and perhaps the courage to speak with unlocked hearts, that we do not know at all that it is the same with others."[3] One of the gifts of being a psychotherapist is that you find that it *is* the same with others. I've traveled the path of transformation myself and with dozens of patients whose pain and courage have deeply affected my understanding of the journey, of my life, and of my faith. Moreover, I have discovered that the Exodus story of the ancient Israelites lights the road we tread when we, too, begin the journey of deep psychological change.

I hope you will make the same discovery as you read the pages of this book. Come and see!

Susan Davis, Ph.D.
Redwood City, California
May 2011

---

[3] Sheldon Vanauken, *A Severe Mercy*, (San Francisco: Harper Collins, 1977), p. 238. He is pondering why so many were touched by so personal a story as his.

The big question is whether you are going to be able to say a hearty yes to your adventure . . . . the adventure of the hero— the adventure of being alive.
Joseph Campbell

Chapter One:
Transformation, the Hero's Adventure

I never thought I'd be here. Never expected this. Don't want it. Yet here I am, walking down from the Sinai—of my own free will—back into Egypt. Well, my own free will? Yes, but with that strange experience a few weeks ago, things have somehow shifted for me. I see more clearly now. It doesn't mean I'm not afraid. I know fear—of death by sword or serpent, of loneliness so great it chokes, of meaning nothing and belonging nowhere—and I am afraid now of all those things. But Zipporah was right, as she so often is. She said, "When God speaks to you, what choice do you have? All roads but his are lesser things, and your soul knows it." She said, "Moses, you must go."

Egypt. I see it lying green and fertile before me, delta of the life-giving Nile. It is the land of my birth, yet somehow never home. I am going down to challenge Ramses, whom they call the Great.[4] I know him well,

---

[4] Dating the Exodus during the period from 1250-1200 BC places Moses' lifetime concurrent with the pharaoh of that period. Though debated for decades, the consensus of modern biblical archeological scholarship suggests this time period for the Exodus and thus reinforces the popular tradition that names Ramses II, who reigned over Egypt from 1279-1213 BC, as this biblical pharaoh.

grew up with him. Stubborn and proud, from birth held divine, nothing denied him. He has intelligence, but of a crafty kind, schooled in the intrigues of the court, the priests. This will not be easy.

I am going down to set my people free. That's what the voice said from the bush that did not burn: "I have heard the suffering of my people in Egypt. I intend to set my people free." My people, my mother and brothers and sisters, descendents of Jacob called Israel, groaning in slavery, abused and shamed, neglected and used. Yes, that is a worthy goal, an honorable task. It disturbs but it also thrills me. The ember of outrage, so long banked under deep ashes, was fanned by those flames that did not consume, aroused by the voice calling my name. It is glowing now, ready to burst into flame. So I am afraid of myself. I am afraid I am not able to carry out this task, but I am more afraid of that flame within me. It has been destructive before, destroyed a life, and then destroyed the life I had. Yes, that is the deeper truth. I am less afraid of my death or my weakness than I am afraid of my anger and my power, a consuming fire. But when God speaks to you, what choice do you have?

Let us go.

~~~~~~~

So we might imagine Moses as he stood on the cusp of a choice and an adventure, both for himself and for the people of Israel. His choice—returning to Egypt to accomplish an impossible and beautiful task because he heard a voice and saw a mystery—was the beginning of a story that has molded human history.

Stories can be powerful things, and human beings are story-telling, story-loving people. "Let me tell you a story" is an irresistible invitation for young and old, regardless of such incidentals as history or culture. Stories are how we make sense of our world, our lives, and each other, and stories are how we remember. Stories have been chanted, written, filmed, sung, acted, mimed, and you could even say that the thoughts going on inside our heads are the stories we tell ourselves. History, psychology, art and literature, holy Scripture—all stories. In the pages that follow, we will explore many stories: biblical stories of the Exodus and of Jesus' death and resurrection, clinical stories of some of my patients[5], bits of my own story, psychological stories or theories, and stories told by artists in poetry and literature.

The Exodus journey of the children of Israel has served as a core metaphor or story for both Judaism and Christianity and is also embraced by Islam. It has been told and retold around campfires and Sabbath dinner tables, from pulpits and in the writings of monks and mystics[6] for more than three thousand years. Its power to fire the human imagination and feed the soul comes from the truth it tells of a universal process of deep transformation—one we may seek, or one we may try to avoid; one that lights our individual paths toward wholeness. Its message is as important and current today as it has been for millennia.

My own interest in the deep truth of the Exodus story was sparked by one of my patients. Depressed and anxious, Joanna[7] was caught in repetitive patterns of personal and professional relationships in which she found herself ambivalent, passive, and passive-aggressive. She felt "stuck in the muck," neither giving her all nor moving on. Perhaps most painful was her exquisitely attuned awareness of

---

[5] In choosing the stories of my patients, I will share only a few of the many I could have chosen, largely randomly as their journeys have coincided with my writing of a chapter. I use their stories with their permission and in ways that maintain their confidentiality. Names and details have been changed, but quotations are as I have reconstructed them from the notes I have taken during our therapy work together.

[6] I am grateful to Robert Hamerton-Kelly, who pointed out this connection to the writing of Philo of Alexandria and the writer known as Pseudodionysius.

[7] This name has, as have all the client names you will see in these pages, been changed to protect confidentiality.

3

her own emotional and psychological state. One day she returned from celebrating Passover and said, "The children of Israel went to Egypt for security and it became their slavery. Where is *my* internal Moses?"

Joanna was using the Exodus story to understand what was happening in her own life. Her comment opened broad avenues of thought for me about the Exodus story as a journey of transformative change. How often do we find ourselves in circumstances or patterns of behavior that began for security but ultimately became a kind of slavery? Do we each have elements within us that can lead us into new freedom and new life? What are the signposts guiding us through that journey of deep transformation? Are there predictable stages in the journey? The Exodus story points us toward true and practical answers to each of these questions, answers we will explore in the pages that follow. Let's get an overview of the journey now.

The Stages of the Transformative Journey

Whether it starts with a dream, a symptom such as depression or panic, or an external circumstance such as a tragic accident, the general outlines of the transformative journey are universal and proceed in predictable ways. Moreover, the same process takes place in individuals, relationships and families, organizations and political systems, and cultures—and one level affects the others. It is deep—affecting us both spiritually and psychologically—and fundamentally restructures the way we organize ourselves and, sometimes, our lives. Though we may long for transformative change and the wholeness and freedom it offers, we usually fear and resist it. Though it is of such fundamental importance that Scripture, poetry, self-help books, and psychotherapy research all explore it, we don't fully understand it. When we are in the midst of it, it can be frightening and seem the opposite of the gift that it is.

As Joanna had pointed out, it began in Egypt. The family of a man named Jacob, who came to be known as Israel, went to Egypt to survive a region-wide famine. Four hundred years later his descendants had become the slaves of the Egyptians. How often we adopt ways of being in the world in order to survive one situation only to find that we are stuck and creating problems for ourselves in others. **Stage One: Egypt**—when security and safety become slavery.

It is difficult to break out of slavery—at times even difficult to *want* to break out. The familiar and known, though it may be uncomfortable and sometimes actually destructive, exerts a powerful influence. How then do we come to change at all? Moses encountered the burning bush. The Egyptians and Israelites experienced plagues: frogs and boils and the angel of death. **Stage Two: Burning Bushes and Plagues**. In our safe slavery, we find ourselves disturbed and troubled by forces within us—psychological and spiritual—or outside us—the external circumstances we often do not choose and may not even deserve.

Stage Three: The Red Sea. Here Moses and the Israelites were camped on the shores of a shallow inland sea. They had begun their journey by leaving Egypt, but Pharaoh's chariots were in pursuit. Ahead lay a desert wilderness, barren and dry. They were frightened and had to choose to go back to Egypt or forward into the unknown. The Red Sea represents a decision point, something often called a leap of faith. Shall we go back to what is familiar, or forward into the unknown?

"Tell the Israelites to go forward!"[8] So God commanded and so the people chose. The waters parted and the people went through, but they did not walk straight to the Promised Land. **Stage Four: Wandering in the Wilderness**. They needed time to regroup, to

---

[8] Exodus 14:15, New Revised Standard Version (NRSV)

develop a new identity as a free people, new ways of being in the world and with each other, a new understanding of reality and a new experience of the presence of God. When they were ready they would be able to enter the Promised Land and remain true to what they had learned.

Stage Five: The Promised Land. The children of Israel finally entered into a new land, one filled with giants to be conquered, but one flowing with milk and honey. This is the stage in which we are ready, having left the old and learned something new, to implement our new ways of being in the world. We can create new outcomes, conquer our fears, and take possession of new and fulfilling areas of our lives and our relationships. We have become increasingly better armed for life, more whole. "Become increasingly better" is a good description of what happens through the transformative journey. The journey does not lead us to an ending but to new beginnings, not to stasis, but to the opportunity for greater scope and further growth. Ironically, we become something new and yet at the same time more truly ourselves than we have ever been.

Dreams and Killer Whales

Transformation began in my own life without my conscious decision and even against my will—at the juncture between graduate school and my career as a psychologist, between youth and middle age, on an island in the middle of the Pacific Ocean—with a nightmare. I sat bolt upright, alone in my bed, not exactly afraid but absolutely alert. Later that day, in supervision for my pre-doctoral internship at the Queen's Medical Center in Honolulu, I discussed a young Filipino with a C-2 level spinal cord injury. He'd be on a respirator and probably warehoused in a care facility for the rest of his life. I thought of my dream and found myself sobbing. The world seemed such a dangerous place. My supervisors suggested psychotherapy . . . . for me.

In my first session with René Tillich, Ph.D.—brilliant clinical psychologist known on the island as a master therapist and therapist to therapists—he asked, "What brings you?" I told him my dream:

> *I was swimming in a pool with small, butterfly-like tropical fish. Suddenly the dream shifted, and I was no longer in the pool. I heard that killer whales were breeding in the North Atlantic. Now confined to a small bay, they would destroy humankind if they were allowed to continue. With alarm and anxiety, I was putting their mothball-like eggs into test tubes with stoppers, but they were hatching anyway. I took a huge knife and began cutting the hatchlings—they looked like sardine fillets—in half.*
>
> *Suddenly, two full-size killer whales stood in front of me. One had the head of a baby, and he asked me, "Why are you killing us?" And I didn't know why.*

There are a lot of biologically incorrect images in this dream, but that was not what disturbed me most. The truth is that if someone had offered me a kiss from Shamu the Killer Whale, at this time in my life I would have preferred death. On my first trip to Hawaii, I had discovered to my horror that I had a phobia about swimming with the fishes. This was pretty inconvenient since I loved the tropical waters and even loved the beauty of the fishes—in theory. Now I had a year to live on the island of Oahu, surrounded by those waters and scared of those fishes! If that weren't enough, here I was dreaming of them.

René asked, "In the dream, what part of you is trying to be born? What part of yourself are you having to kill off to keep the world safe?" I said, "I don't know. That's why I'm here." René could dive into the depths of those unconscious waters in ways that terrified me. I am forever grateful for his deep chuckle of delight and his robust belief in the goodness of what would emerge in our work from the unconscious in general and my psyche in particular. I'll say more about this dream and the journey it launched in the next chapter. For now, let's just say that at that moment, like Moses stepping down toward Egypt, René and I stepped out together on my path of transformative change.

An Invitation to Adventure and to Wholeness

The story of Exodus as a transformative journey is not just an interesting idea contained in a dusty old religious book. It belongs to a class of powerful, deeply true stories—stories that may contain but absolutely transcend historicity and verifiable fact. Such stories could be called parables or myths. In a fascinating set of interviews on National Public Radio, Bill Moyers discussed the meaning and value of these sorts of stories with Joseph Campbell, scholar of comparative mythology.[9] Moyers asked a question arising from our common everyday use of the word "myth":

> Bill Moyers said, "But people ask, isn't a myth a lie?"
>
> Joseph Campbell replied, "No, mythology is not a lie; mythology is poetry. It is metaphorical. It has been well said that mythology is the penultimate truth—penultimate because the ultimate cannot be put into words. It is beyond words, beyond images ... Mythology pitches the mind ... to what can be known but not told. So this is the penultimate truth."[10]

---

[9] Joseph Campbell with Bill Moyers, *The Power of Myth*, ed. Betty Sue Flowers (New York: Doubleday, 1988).
[10] Ibid. p. 161

Poetry, story, and metaphor are the right vehicles for truths that can be touched but not grasped. Campbell calls such truths penultimate: "next to the last," the closest we can come before the truths are so large that our vision cannot take them in, our minds cannot encompass them. As we live with such stories, tell them and retell them perhaps for many years, they reveal more and more of those larger truths, layer by layer, enriching and enlarging our perceptions over time.

Moreover, as Joanna recognized, stories with the power of penultimate truth, stories like the Exodus story, transcend their time and shed light on our lives and experience. They bring us something very personal and very current—and if this is true, they are also invitations to an adventure—for us.

> Joseph Campbell said, "The big question is whether you are going to be able to say a hearty yes to your adventure."
>
> Bill Moyers asked, "The adventure of the hero?"
>
> To which Campbell replied, "Yes, the adventure of the hero—the adventure of being alive."[11]

When Moses stepped from the Sinai toward Egypt, he said "yes" to his adventure and began the hero's journey. That journey began a process of transformation for the man Moses, as we shall see in chapter four. Moreover, that "yes" has echoed through history. It has changed the direction of countless lives, of communities, and even of cultures. When I told René "that is why I am here," though I did not know it, I was saying "yes" to my own adventure and beginning my own transformative journey.

[11] Ibid. p. 163.

The transformative process *is* the hero's journey. It is the journey toward becoming what St. Irenaeus of Lyons called the "glory of God": a human being fully alive.[12] The story of the Exodus teaches us that no matter where we start the journey, we can become whole and fully alive—"something rich and strange," as Shakespeare wrote in his last and perhaps greatest play, *The Tempest.* As this play begins, the spirit Ariel sings to the young hero, Ferdinand, suggesting that his father is drowned and lying at the bottom of the sea:

> Full fathom five thy father lies;
> Of his bones are coral made;
> Those are pearls that were his eyes:
> Nothing of him that doth fade
> But doth suffer a sea-change
> Into something rich and strange. [13]

These lines suggest that in our own transformative journeys, what appears like dying may be the beginning of new life and wholeness. The story of the Exodus lights the path that must be trod to accomplish our own "sea-change" and teaches the stages of the transformative process. Let's dust it off, chip away at the old perceptions that encrust it in our minds, and see what we discover.

---

[12] St. Irenaeus of Lyons, in his great work *Against Heresies*, written about 185 A.D., excerpted and read in the Roman Office of Readings on his feast day, June 28.
[13] William Shakespeare, *The Tempest. Act I. Sc. 2.*

"Things don't fall apart. Things hold.
Lines connect in thin ways that last and last
and lives become generations
made out of pictures and words just kept."
Lucille Clifton

"Sainthood is the result of wholeness, not goodness."
Robert Johnson

Chapter Two:
The Generations That Come Before

In her memoir, *Good Woman*, African American poet Lucille Clifton tells stories about the lives of the five generations of her family, beginning with Caroline, born in Africa in 1823. In the end, she writes,

> And I could tell you about things we been through, some awful ones, some wonderful, but I know that the things that make us are more than that, our lives are more than the days in them, our lives are our line and we go on. I type that and I swear I can see Ca'line standing in the green of Virginia, in the green of Afrika, and I swear she makes no sound, but she nods her head and smiles.[14]

---

[14] Lucille Clifton, *Good Woman: Poems and a Memoir*, (Rochester, New York: BOA Editions, Ltd., 1987), p. 276.

And again, beautifully, "Things don't fall apart. Things hold. Lines connect in thin ways that last and last and lives become generations made out of pictures and words just kept."[15] For better or worse, whether relationships are broken or continue, we are inextricably connected to the family tree. Prior generations in our family history write the foreword, whether we have read it or not, to our own life stories. My dream of killer whales that would destroy the world and the nature of my particular Egypt did not come out of the blue. They were rooted in my family dynamics and my family's history, as we will see. All of our stories begin with the family themes that form our psychological, spiritual, and cultural heritages. We are each part of a generational chain in which we are influenced by the choices of those who have come before, and in our turn influence our children and our children's children for generations to come.

The Israelites who found themselves enslaved in Egypt were also influenced by the choices of their ancestors. So let us begin before the beginning, in a sort of preamble to the Exodus story proper, with the story of how the Israelites got to Egypt in the first place. That story's hero is Joseph, eleventh son of Jacob, son of Isaac, son of Abraham. Joseph's life was shaped by his family history and he shaped that history forever after. As we shall see, the complex interplay of Joseph's family history and his own choices brought the children of Israel to Egypt for security in the first place. Joseph's story wonderfully illustrates where the transformative journey begins—with the generations that come before.

Abraham's Dynasty Founded

When he was seventy-five years old, Abraham received a call and a promise from God, "Leave your country, your family, and your father's home for a land that I will show you. I'll make you a great

---

[15] Ibid. p. 275.

nation and bless you . . . All the families of the Earth will be blessed by you."[16] So Abraham took his beautiful wife Sarah and left his home country to strike out for a new life.

As Abraham traveled through the lands of the Middle East, he became very wealthy in herds and property, but he did not have a child though God had assured him that "a son from your body will be your heir."[17] And while Abraham believed God, the years continued and still Sarah was childless. Finally, Sarah hatched a plan to give Abraham a son from his body—but not hers. She offered Abraham her Egyptian maid as a surrogate mother. Abraham complied with her suggestion and took Hagar to bed. She became pregnant with the boy who would be called Ishmael, but when she knew she was pregnant Hagar began to look down on her infertile mistress. Finally, Sarah could take it no more. Hurt and angry, blaming Abraham for the humiliation she now felt, she began to abuse and humiliate Hagar.

Thirteen years passed in this uncomfortable state as Ishmael grew. Abraham was ninety-nine years old when God spoke again, reiterating his promise and his blessing. Abraham had a strong reaction. He "fell flat on his face. And then he laughed, thinking 'Can a hundred-year-old man father a son? And can Sarah, at ninety years, have a baby?'"[18] He asked God to bless Ishmael, and God agreed, but then clarified his intention: Sarah would have a son, Isaac (whose name means 'laughter'), and God would continue his special relationship with Abraham through him.

It happened as God had promised: Sarah did become pregnant and she did bear a beloved son. What began as the derisive laughter of

---

[16] Genesis 12:1-3. This quotation is taken, as are all biblical quotations in this book unless otherwise noted, from *The Message*, Eugene H. Peterson, (Colorado Springs: NavPress, 2002).

[17] Genesis 15:4

[18] Genesis 17:17

disbelief became the laughter of unexpected joy. Yet the tensions in the household did not relent. The jealous rivalry between Sarah and Hagar, now focused on the protection of their sons, continued and worsened until finally Sarah asked Abraham to send Hagar and her young son away. And Abraham, who had tolerated Sarah's abuse of Hagar for so long, again complied with his wife's plan.

> He got up early the next morning, got some food together and a canteen of water for Hagar, put them on her back and sent her away with the child. She wandered off into the desert of Beersheba. When the water was gone, she left the child under a shrub and went off, fifty yards or so. She said, "I can't watch my son die." As she sat, she broke into sobs.[19]

God rescued Ishmael and Hagar, calming and reassuring her and, practically, pointing out a well she had not seen. Ishmael grew up in the desert with his mother, becoming a skilled archer and eventually taking a wife from Egypt. As the biblical account continues, we find that Hagar and her son not only survived this life-threatening excommunication from the family, but continued in some sort of relationship to Abraham. We discover that Ishmael and Isaac were both present to bury their father,[20] but Abraham continued to show preference for Isaac, leaving him all that he owned with only a token gift for his other offspring.[21] The family relationships had clearly continued, but they bore the wounds of the favoritism and life-threatening abandonment that grew from Sarah's jealousy and Abraham's passive compliance.

Ironically for this family specially chosen by God, the terror of not being chosen came to haunt Abraham's family. In the moment in

---

[19] Genesis 21:14–18
[20] Genesis 25:9
[21] Genesis 25:5-6

which Abraham and Sarah sent Hagar and Ishmael away, not being chosen nearly became fatal, as the deep human fear of abandonment became a real possibility in the family of Abraham.

Abraham's Great-Grandson: Joseph

These themes of favoritism, rivalry, and abandonment—and the anger, betrayal, competition, and deceit resulting from them—were played out in the generations that followed Abraham and Sarah, in their son Isaac's family, and in his son Jacob's family, too.[22] As his story begins, Joseph—eleventh of Jacob's twelve sons—had become his father's favorite.

> Israel loved Joseph more than any of his other sons because he was the child of his old age. And he made him an elaborately embroidered coat. When his brothers realized that their father loved him more than them, they grew to hate him—they wouldn't even speak to him.[23]

The hatred and jealousy of Joseph's brothers grew, and Joseph played his own part in feeding it. He tattled on his brothers, seeking to align himself with his father and to set his father against his brothers. He showed off his beautiful coat, evidence of his place as favorite. He shared dreams in which all of his family members bowed down to him.[24] The apple of both parents' eyes, perhaps the child Joseph had learned to gain their praise and pleasure, to secure his place as chosen and beloved, by sharing stories of his prowess and accomplishment, of his dreams and ambitions. You might imagine a boy today, bragging about his excellent grades, crowing over the points he

---

[22] See the stories in Genesis 25, 27, and 30.
[23] Genesis 37:3-4
[24] Genesis 37:5-11

scored at soccer, shouting "Hey, look at me!" as he balanced at the top of the high dive.

But by this time Joseph was seventeen years old and not a naïve child. His dreams suggest that he had intuitively recognized the family pattern of competition and struggle for preference and power, the extreme importance of being chosen and honored as favorite. His behaviors and his dreams suggest that he was actively seeking and courting his position as favorite. Eventually even his parents felt the dreams were a bit much.[25]

Dysfunctional family patterns, childhood problems and solutions, become hard habits hard to break. Joseph tried to maintain his place as cherished favorite in the context of a family system riddled with the fear of not being chosen and the power struggles and jealousy that result from it. Joseph and his family were stuck in a pattern of behavior that not only represented a kind of slavery but that held the seeds of its own destruction. Family patterns contribute to the beginning point of every transformative process: the familiar but problematic place we are describing with the Exodus metaphor of slavery in Egypt.

Joseph's brothers' jealousy and resentment finally boiled over. They decided to get rid of him altogether—through death if necessary. Luckily, a caravan was passing by. Instead of killing him, they sold their brother into slavery in Egypt. The worst had happened: Joseph was not chosen but cast out, not favorite but lost and unknown, not first but least and last.

Joseph's fortunes had fallen very low. They would rise and fall and rise again in Egypt—as he sought solace in the God of his fathers Abraham, Isaac, and Jacob, and sought to replace his earlier jockeying for position with a new integrity and capacity for service

[25] See Genesis 38.

and responsibility. In the end, through his skill as an interpreter of dreams, Joseph rose to become Pharaoh's chief minister, preparing Egypt through years of prosperity for the years of famine that would soon engulf the entire region.

Eventually, the chosen but dysfunctional family of Abraham, living in the land of Canaan, was drawn into the famine. Driven by hunger, Jacob sent his older sons to Egypt for food. What follows is one of the most moving reunions in Scripture. It happened during the second trip the brothers made to Egypt, this time bringing Joseph's beloved younger brother Benjamin with them. Accused of stealing a valuable cup that Joseph himself had planted in Benjamin's bag, the brothers were hauled back for judgment before him. Joseph demanded that Benjamin be left behind as his slave in punishment for the crime, but his brother, Judah, pleaded:

> "Your servant, my father, told us, 'You know very well that my wife gave me two sons. One turned up missing. I concluded that he'd been ripped to pieces. I've never seen him since. If you now go and take this one and something bad happens to him, you'll put my old gray, grieving head in the grave for sure.'
>
> So let me stay here as your slave, not this boy. Let the boy go back with his brothers. How can I go back to my father if the boy is not with me? Oh, don't make me go back and watch my father die in grief!"[26]

Whatever his plan to secure Benjamin to himself had been, Joseph was now deeply moved. He sent his servants away. He broke into gut-wrenching sobs, and when he could speak again, he told them who he was. Now it was their turn to be unable to speak. He embraced them and sent them back to gather Jacob and their families and

---

[26] Genesis 44:27-29, 33-34

possessions to bring them back to Egypt. As he was to reassure them years later when Jacob died and their fears of his retribution resurfaced, he explained, "Don't you see, you planned evil against me but God used those same plans for my good, as you see all around you right now—life for many people."[27]

As a result of his own transformative journey, Joseph could be used for good to bring life for many people. When he had his brothers more than in his power—when he could have taken revenge and abandoned them to death, when he could have re-established his place in his father's affections with absolute impunity, when he would have been more than justified in punishing and rejecting them—he broke with the family pattern. Instead of casting his brothers out, Joseph took them in. Jacob and his sons came to live in Egypt with Joseph. They survived the years of famine and prospered in the good land Joseph arranged for them.

Abraham and Sarah's family history shows us how what is unresolved by earlier generations becomes the burden of the next generation. Family patterns become part of real problems that we each must find a way to solve, whether we are consciously aware of them or not. Let's continue to look at the generational inheritance that contributes to all of our lives, particularly to our personal Egypts, through the lens of psychology.

A Psychological Idea: Multigenerational Transmission

One of Sigmund Freud's great contributions to humankind was the recognition that psychological symptoms do not arise in a vacuum or as a visitation from God in punishment for sin. He saw that there were real relational contexts within which these problems arose. His famous Oedipal complex is such a context: the adult patient's

[27] Genesis 50:20

symptoms are related to childhood traumatic hurt or developmental challenges in the context of his parents' early relationships with each other and with him. Freud saw that there was meaning in the symptom, and that healing could begin when that meaning was explored and understood. It is sometimes difficult from our vantage point in history to appreciate how radical and rich this insight was.

There was tremendous excitement in the fields of psychology and psychoanalysis as Freud's ideas revolutionized thinking about and treatment of mental disorders and emotional suffering, but by the mid 1900s, psychoanalysts and psychologists had run aground on the recalcitrant problem of schizophrenia. With its tormented emotions and twisted thoughts, schizophrenia did not yield to the "talking cure" Freud had discovered.[28]

So some psychologists and psychoanalysts began to experiment with new ways to help schizophrenics and their families. Murray Bowen was one of this creative new breed of therapist. He began with the assumption, then current, that problems in the mother-child relationship caused the problems of schizophrenia. So he tried hospitalizing the schizophrenic patient together with family members for months at a time. He began to observe that problems and patterns in families were not confined to the parent-child relationship or even to the immediate nuclear family group.[29]

"Multigenerational transmission" was the term he coined to describe how family interactional and emotional patterns tend to repeat themselves across generations. Early marriages or multiple divorces, mother-daughter closeness or father-son competitiveness, weak men

---

[28] We now understand that schizophrenia is the result of a complex interplay of physiological and emotional stresses, with an emphasis on the genetic predisposition of an individual to the disorder.

[29] While schizophrenia is not caused by family interactions, rooted as it is in genetic codes, volatile and hostile emotional relationships can influence its severity.

and strong women or dependent women with caretaking men—all these patterns and a myriad of others were discovered as Bowen and later colleagues[30] began to explore family histories.

This idea may help us understand what it means when, in Exodus 34:7, Moses describes God as "keeping steadfast love for the thousandth generation . . . but visiting the iniquity of the parents upon the children and the children's children, to the third and the fourth generation."[31] This is less a statement about God's judgment and more a statement of observed fact. We can see it occurring in Joseph's life and also in our own. It is part of each of our legacies: family strengths and family weaknesses, family courage and family fear, patterns of light and darkness, the choices of individuals in prior generations affecting the lives of their descendents.

Strange and even unfair as it may seem, multigenerational transmission suggests that Abraham's passive compliance and Sarah's wish to send Hagar and Ishmael away—her jealousy, her angry insistence on her primacy in the household hierarchy—are linked to their great-grandson Joseph being sold into slavery by his brothers. Joseph's choices in Egypt—to humble himself, to honor his God and his masters, to forgive and receive his brothers back into loving family relationship—saved his family from a famine as well as from a pattern of destructive relationships that had plagued generations.

Multigenerational transmission does not determine our personal choices, but it does affect the hand we are dealt and must play for ourselves. It shapes the patterns that bind us, our Egypts—of the fears we must face at points of decision, our Red Seas—and of the hopes

---

[30] Monica McGoldrick and Edwin Friedman were among those to take this idea and develop it using a sort of psychological family tree, a tool termed the "genogram."
[31] New Revised Standard Version

that lead us toward our personal Promised Lands. Understanding our own family histories can enable us to recognize Egypt and to map our course through the wilderness. Finding the Promised Land represents, as Joseph discovered, life for many people—our loved ones today as well as generations to come.

Let's turn to a modern example of such multigenerational transmission, one very close to home.

Chaos, Christ, and Killer Whales

My dream of killer whales that could destroy the world took place in just such a multigenerational context. The dream reveals my Egypt: a preoccupation with safety and security, and a fear of the destructive power of what lies beneath the surface of the psyche. That fear was symbolized by killer whales that dove and rose from deep beneath the cold dark waters of the Atlantic. Though my family legacy is one of courage and faith, it is also one of fear. We have had the courage to seek new lands and new lives. We have loved and laughed and learned, but we have also feared the dark underbelly of our humanity, the irrational and unpredictable, the anger and hurt and hunger for love that lay buried and disowned within us. Woven through my family's stories are themes of light and darkness, of religious faith used as a bulwark against the pain that can result from human passion. Those themes were writ large in my parents' growing up years and finally, through their marriage, in mine.

The second of three girls, my mother remembers her dad's fun and laughter, but also his rigid and uncompromising punishment of wrongdoing. When she crawled under the bed to cut off her unfashionable braids, he laughed and made an appointment at the beauty parlor, but when she punched a love-crazed boy in the nose for teasing her about wetting her pants in kindergarten, her father's belt was ready and stinging while he lectured, "Christians do not get angry!" When she tossed her detested split pea soup out the home economics classroom window (unfortunately onto the head of the school janitor) he marched her in front of her entire seventh grade class to apologize. My grandparents' home was not without love, but it was rigidly ordered. Barriers were erected against the irrationality and unpredictability of anger and sexual passion. Yet these barriers failed to hold, even for my grandfather. In high school, my mother burst into her father's church office to find lipstick on his face, his glasses in his hand, and the church choir director smoothing her skirt.

If my mother's home was rigidly ordered, my father's was awash with all too much passion and unpredictability. His mother had bipolar disorder in the days before lithium made its wild mood swings manageable. When, at seven years old, my dad ran into the living room to cling to the arm his father had raised to strike his mother in an alcoholic rage, his father walked out of the house and never came back. The boy believed it was all his fault. It was not until Dad became the local high school football hero that he saw his father again, sitting in the bleachers.

Meanwhile, his mother's mood disorder resulted not only in periods of withdrawal and depression, but also in chaotic, playful, manic days and unpredictable weeks away from her children. One Christmas Eve, his aunt arrived to take two small children to buy a Christmas tree while their mother was staying in a sanitarium. In those years, as is so easy for a single parent to do, his mother chose her only son as a surrogate husband. She was flirtatious, dependent, and intrusive at times—irritably rejecting or lost in depression at others.

When Jim Rayburn, a young Presbyterian minister, came to West Dallas High to found his first Young Life Club, Dad experienced belonging, security, and clarity for the first time. He met Jim when delivering his newspaper. Jim recognized a lonely, insecure boy, and would wait on the front steps for Dad to come by on his paper route and have a chat. Eventually Dad chose, as had my mother's parents, to ground himself amidst the chaos of his parents' emotional problems and the unpredictability and loneliness of his childhood on the rock of faith.

My parents fell madly in love when they met as undergraduates at Whitworth College in Spokane, Washington. My father found in my mother the same sense of belonging, security, and clarity that had first attracted him to faith. She found in him a masculine power, a zest for life, and an attractive rebellion against the strict moral code of her missionary parents. They went to movies. They smooched under the pine trees that dotted the campus. They married and had five kids.

They did not live happily ever after. Their mutual fear of what lay beneath the surface of the psyche—its dark longing, passion, and anger—and their mutual effort to avoid it through religious faith did not hold. He succumbed to that which he had split off and had been unable to acknowledge. As his bipolar mother had lived out two different selves, a light side and a dark one, so did he. Charming and attractive, he preached and pastored. With unhealed pain and old repressed anger, he found himself slipping into the dark world of sexual addiction. Unable to confront him or to leave him— "Christians don't get angry"—my mother felt deeply inadequate, losing much of her playfulness and passion even as she clung more tightly to her faith.

So my brothers and sisters and I grew up in a sunny household that had real darkness split off and held beneath the surface. We played hide and seek with the neighbor kids and got books to read from the library. We dove into the cool green waters of Flathead Lake and sang by the campfire as sparks flew up to the stars. We posed with our red felt and sequined Christmas stockings for the yearly photographs that charted our growth, and we learned to uphold that split before we were even conscious that it existed.

Yet it could not be upheld. The darkness began to leak out even as I, the oldest, left for college. With all the light and warmth and life that religious faith brings, it can become a sort of slavery if it is used rigidly to defend against human longing and passion, the unconscious and the unpredictable. Religion is then used in the service of psychological defenses, not of the God who is doing something brand-new. It can be used to divide and to hide, especially from aspects of ourselves—our feelings, our needs, our perceptions—that don't fit or that threaten what we want to be or believe we should be. But what is repressed is not inert. The more rigidly we split the darkness and the light, the more likely the darkness will break through that barrier, and the more destructive it will be when it does.

In my senior year of college, I dreamt of *a witch, burrowing under my mother's house. Mom and I were standing beside her hole, watching her legs and feet disappear into the ground. I couldn't understand why Mom was not exorcizing the witch, but instead stood by like a zombie. I began to utter the words of exorcism.* The dream reminded me of the scene in the movie *The Wizard of Oz.*[32] It terrified me as a child when the witch's legs shriveled up and disappeared under Dorothy's house. I must have felt the dangerously undermining trouble in my home and my mother's inability to cope with it. The dream showed the split between what appears on the surface and what lies under the surface, between the words of exorcism—"in the name of Jesus . . ."—and the destructive and dynamic power of the witch, between the light of faith and reason and the feared darkness of human passions.

---

[32] This 1939 film, directed by Victor Fleming and starring Judy Garland, was based on the novel by L. Frank Baum entitled, *The Wonderful Wizard of Oz.*

Caught in compulsions, afraid of his own wounding and rage, the retaining wall of religion collapsing, his marriage, family, and profession deeply threatened though yet intact—my dad died suddenly after hip replacement surgery when he was fifty-two years old and I was twenty-eight.[33] Mom, thrust abruptly from her secure but painful Egypt, stunned and emotionally bruised, entered therapy to begin her own transformational journey. She began graduate school, became a psychologist and a psychotherapist. She learned how—in the imagery of my dream—to utter the words of exorcism she could not say before, to bring the dynamic transformational power of the unconscious and of the spiritual into contact, to heal the split.

So my killer whale dream did not come out of the blue, but carried the weight of my family's struggle against the chaos and unpredictability of the irrational side of our humanity. It carried the fear of passions that had been repressed into the unconscious. It carried the longing for wholeness and authenticity of self and relationship that had been denied in the name of safety and security. It forced me, as did Joseph's shocking shift from favorite son to outcast, to confront the family patterns and problems that enslaved me and hurt my loved ones. Our solution of splitting rational from irrational through religious faith did not hold and could not hold. It was inherently flawed. What is repressed is not inert but, like a powerful killer whale, it rises from the dark depths to leap and breach and make itself known.

So what are we to do? I have been surprised to learn that God's voice can be heard through the irrational when we open to the unconscious. God is on the side of wholeness and love and new life,

---

[33] I wonder if his death was his unconscious resolution of the deep conflict he felt as well as a loving, if perhaps cowardly, way to protect his loved ones from further pain. The mind and body are inextricably linked in mysterious ways. If so, perhaps that was his Red Sea choice and the beginning of a transformative process that goes beyond my human understanding. I do hope and pray that this is so.

and in the service of these goals, God is not afraid—as we are—of our human darkness. As King David the psalmist reminds us,

> Is there anyplace I can go to avoid your Spirit?
> to be out of your sight? . . .
> It's a fact: darkness isn't dark to you;
> night and day, darkness and light, they're all the same to you.[34]

Dappled Things and the Goal of Transformation

Centuries after David wrote his psalm, another poet and man of faith shared this insight that God is not afraid of our human darkness. Instead, he says, God is on the side of "dappled things," and not of keeping dark split from light. Is it possible that within what we deem dark and unacceptable there is something God can redeem and use for great goodness and glory? "The stone the masons discarded as flawed is now the capstone!"[35]

This is Gerard Manley Hopkins' poem:

Pied Beauty

Glory be to God for dappled things—
For skies of couple-colour as a brinded cow;
For rose-moles all in stipple upon trout that swim;
Fresh-firecoal chestnut-falls; finches' wings;
Landscape plotted and pieced—fold, fallow, and plough;
And all trades, their gear and tackle and trim.
All things counter, original, spare, strange;
Whatever is fickle, freckled (who knows how?)
With swift, slow; sweet, sour; adazzle, dim;

---

[34] Psalm 139:7-12
[35] Psalm 118:22

He fathers-forth whose beauty is past change:
Praise him.[36]

Whenever I think of this poem, I remember standing under an old wisteria vine in Palo Alto during a partial eclipse of the sun some years ago. The shadows cast by the leafy vine each had the shape of a crescent moon, thousands of half moons dappling the grass and walkway beneath. It is an image of the interpenetration of light and dark—neither unshadowed light nor unlit darkness—and represents to me the beginning of transformation and the integration of opposites that bring wholeness. Notice the homey images Hopkins uses in his poem: jersey cows and spotted trout and house finches, farmland and the tools of the trades, and perhaps Chinese sweet-and-sour pork! Is it possible that we cannot actually be fully human, fully alive, whole and holy, without such integration?

Ironically, though transformation is at the core of the Judeo-Christian tradition and spirituality, people of faith are often, as I was, the ones most frightened of the unknown and of the process of change. We fear that we will lose our faith when, in fact, the opposite is true. We fear the unconscious and the new, though our Scriptures show us again and again a God who rejoices in creative and transformative power. God says,

"Forget about what's happened;
don't keep going over old history.
Be alert, be present. I'm about to do something brand-new.
It's bursting out! Don't you see it?"[37]

---

[36] Gerard Manley Hopkins, "Pied Beauty," from *The Poems of Gerard Manley Hopkins*, ed. W.H. Gardner & N.H. MacKenzie (Oxford: Oxford University Press, 4th edition, 1967), p. 69-70.
[37] Isaiah 43:18-19

We fear that what is in us is bad, or that we will become sinful if we change when, in fact, the process of transformation releases the creative power of wholeness. The dictionary shows the word *holy* is a derivative of the word for *whole* in Old Norse, Old Saxon, Old High German, and Old English.[38] Perhaps our Germanic ancestors knew something profound. In his autobiographical book, *Balancing Heaven and Earth,* Jungian analyst Robert Johnson suggests that seeking wholeness is the essence of the religious life:

> Listening to the will of God as it manifests within your own psyche, hearing what has been called the still, small voice within—this is the religious life. This cannot be reduced to a tidy formula, but one general guideline is to ask yourself what is needed for wholeness in any situation. Instead of asking what is good or what coincides with our personal interest, ask what is whole-making. Sainthood is the result of wholeness, not goodness.[39]

The journey of transformation is an ongoing journey toward integration and wholeness, freedom and freshness, and always requires new ways of being in the world. That means we must inevitably face what we have been afraid of: the apocryphal darkness that lies within. For Joseph, that meant facing the terror that shot through the relationships in Abraham's family, that of being an outcast, one not chosen and even abandoned to death. For me, it has involved facing the dark and unpredictable side of my own unconscious, and with it my anger and my power, my capacity for passion and for play.

---

[38] Webster's College Dictionary, ed. Sol Steinmetz (New York: Random House, 1997), p. 621.
[39] Robert Johnson, *Balancing Heaven and Earth* (San Francisco: HarperCollins Publishers, 1998), p. 101.

In our first psychotherapy session, René said, "Let me share some impressions . . . I'm hearing repeated themes of safety through what you say. Perhaps the part that wants to be born has something to do with play, freedom, rest, adventure. I suspect that it will not destroy the world but will be something very creative and positive."

It has been years now since I first began that adventure, my own Exodus journey toward wholeness. As those who know me can tell you, I am not finished yet! This book has been written to share what I have learned on the journey about the journey. It reflects that very creative and positive thing, that sea-change into something rich and strange, that came into my life from killer whales who destroy old worlds and the God who exults in doing what is brand-new, in fathering forth dappled things, and in planning life for many people.

It is encouraging to me to read Father Thomas Keating's assessment of the transformative journey, one with which I'm sure Joseph would have agreed.

> The journey, or process itself, is what Jesus called the Kingdom of God. This is a very important point. To accept our illness and whatever damage was done to us in life by people or circumstances is to participate in the cross of Christ and in our own redemption. In other words, the acceptance of our wounds is not only the beginning, but the journey itself. It does not matter if we do not finish it. If we are on the journey, we are in the Kingdom.[40]

Let's continue that journey together, where safety and security become slavery, in Egypt.

---

[40] Thomas Keating, *Intimacy with God* (New York: The Crossroad Publishing Co., 2002), p. 90.

We will not be shipwrecked on a vain reality.
Henry David Thoreau

Chapter Three:
When Safety Becomes Slavery

Sarah was a little nervous when she came into my office. It's scary meeting a therapist for the first time—even if you have had that therapist's phone number for a year. She was well dressed, wore a gorgeous diamond ring, and her blonde hair was beautifully cut. She spoke of her three great teenaged kids who were doing well in their exclusive private schools and mentioned their vacation home on Lake Tahoe. She noted her husband's career success and their marriage of eighteen years.

But her heart was broken, her mind confused. She was afraid to leave her children in their father's care. The past weekend the couple's getaway was spoiled when he passed out drunk on the couch. Worse, "I feel like a paid whore. He always wants sex when he's drunk," she sobbed. "I guess I've been enabling him. I'm afraid I'll find out I should leave . . ."

The next week, she reported that things were better. He hadn't gotten drunk, and she was hoping things would be okay. She admitted that she was always hoping things were better, but then he'd be drunk again. She wasn't even sure why she had come in to see me, because she didn't know what to discuss. I said, "Great! I'm so glad things are better and that you don't know what to talk about. Sometimes the best sessions happen when people don't know what to say—more room for us both to be surprised by what you didn't know you wanted to say!" And so our therapy began.

As Sarah's therapist, I didn't know whether she should leave her husband or not, whether he might confront his alcoholism or not, but I knew that she was struggling with a security that had become slavery. I wondered whether she was afraid to shake up her comfortable lifestyle. I knew that she was afraid to disturb her children's lives by divorce, even though she had come to recognize that their lives were deeply disturbed by their father's drunkenness. I knew that she had developed long-standing ways of being in the world and in relationship—of loving by making too many sacrifices and taking too much responsibility, of helping by figuring things out and compensating for others, of believing that things would fall apart if she didn't hold them together. I knew that she would have to change those ways in order for any other change to take place, and I was pretty sure that she had learned those ways of being in the world very early, probably in her earliest relationships with her parents and family. I could see that, painful as her situation was, it was also frightening to consider change.

So many of us can identify with Sarah, perhaps not with her particular Egypt, but with the disappointment of finding ourselves in circumstances that are painful yet familiar and secure and difficult to change. In this chapter, we'll explore how we seek safety in the very real situations in which we find ourselves, especially as children, and how that safety can become our slavery. Our security-become-slavery occurs on two interconnected levels: one is the specific external circumstances and relationships in which we live. The second underlies and powers the first: it is comprised of the ways of coping and being in a relationship, of thinking and feeling, that we developed as children and of which we may be only dimly aware. These are the links in the cross-generational chain: childhood solutions to real problems are lessons learned, internalized, and carried with us that help to create the external realities of our lives.

Let's start by considering how the children of Israel had survived the great regional famine only to find themselves, four hundred years later, slaves to the Egyptians.

The Exodus Story

Though the family of Israel had come to Egypt and survived the famine, both Joseph and his father Jacob, also known as Israel, prophesied that their children would again leave Egypt to return to the land given to their forefather Abraham in Canaan. "Then Joseph made the sons of Israel promise under oath, 'When God makes his visitation, make sure you take my bones with you as you leave here.'"[41] Israel's clan had come to Egypt for survival and for security, but not to stay.

Let's consider the specific strategy Joseph hatched to save his family from the famine in Egypt while preserving their opportunity to survive as a people independent of Egypt—to survive but not to stay. He told Pharaoh they were shepherds—"for Egyptians look down on anyone who is a shepherd."[42] Then he asked for and received the choice land of Goshen. In this way, Joseph ensured that there would be no social pressure or even much opportunity to mix, mingle, and be lost in the larger society of Egypt. It was a brilliant way to cope with a difficult set of circumstances and to enable the family of Israel to maintain its own identity and cohesion as a people and to worship its own God. Unfortunately, this cultivation of an innate prejudice

---

[41] Genesis 50:25
[42] Genesis 46:34

in Egyptian society—genius as it was in the specific problem it solved—ultimately became a problem.

Scholars say that the time between the story that ends in the book of Genesis and the beginning of the events called the Exodus was around four hundred years. [43] In four hundred years, the Israelites had not left Egypt to resettle in Canaan. In four hundred years, the Israelites must have come to consider Egypt home, their familiar place. They knew the language, the customs, the local gossip, and the neighbors. They knew the landscape and the seasons, how the moon cast its light over the Nile, and when to plant their crops. Their houses and children and animals were there. In Egypt, they had been born, perhaps fallen in love, raised their families, and buried their grandparents. Joseph's plan and his people had flourished.

Yet, eventually,

> [a] new king came to power in Egypt who didn't know Joseph. He spoke to his people in alarm, "There are way too many of these Israelites for us to handle. We've got to do something: Let's devise a plan to contain them, lest if there's a war they should join our enemies, or just walk off and leave us."[44]

The Egyptians forced the Israelites into hard labor building cities for Pharaoh. "But the harder the Egyptians worked them the more children the Israelites had—children everywhere! The Egyptians got so they couldn't stand the Israelites and treated them worse than ever, crushing them with slave labor."[45] Then Pharaoh devised a new scheme to control the Israelites. He told the Israelite midwives:

---

[43] See *The Interpreter's Bible*, (Abingdon Press, 1994).
[44] Exodus 1:8-10
[45] Exodus 1:12

"'Every boy that is born, drown him in the Nile. But let the girls live.'"[46]

Why didn't the Israelites leave before it got so bad? Why didn't they follow their forefathers' prophesies and return to Canaan when they could have? Perhaps they had moved from a state of comfort and familiarity into one of oppression and pain so slowly that they barely noticed. Perhaps when they noticed, they did not know what to do and did not think they could do it if they had. People say that you can boil a living frog in a pot of water—if you heat it slowly. If you pop him into hot water, he'll jump out, but if the water is cool and then heated to boiling slowly, he will not recognize what is happening until it is too late. We can empathize with the human tendency to choose what is familiar, ignoring the warning signs of disaster until it's too late.

For the children of Israel, safety and security had quite literally become slavery and, in fact, nearly genocide. The solutions the Israelites had devised to solve their problems became problems in themselves. The first problem developed at the level of external circumstances and relationships. To keep apart from a larger culture does maintain a separate identity, but as a minority gains power it can threaten the larger society. Their different values and cultural mores came to threaten the status quo.

The second problem was a more insidious one. It had to do with internal patterns of thoughts and feelings, of identity and self-concept. Such internal psychological patterns reinforce and are reinforced by what is happening in the outside world. Joseph helped Israel's tribe survive through separation from the larger Egyptian society. Yet, separate because they were looked down on, they maintained their identity but somehow lost their self-esteem. Instead of pride as an independent people, the Israelites' dependence on Egypt lent itself

---

[46] Exodus 1:22

to the slow development of a sort of an inferiority complex, a slave mentality. Perhaps that mentality, combined with the comfort of the familiar, contributed to their inability to react to changing social conditions.

In this sense, the story of the Exodus serves as a powerful metaphor, an allegory, for what happens in each of our lives. We, too, find solutions to problems that threaten our survival, especially in the very real situations that we experience as children. Later, our childhood solutions often actually create adult problems and blind us to the choices we have when circumstances change around us. Like the Israelites, we too find it difficult to leave what is familiar even when it is painful. The reason this happens is fundamental to the development of the human person. Let's consider what psychology tells us about how human beings develop and about the childhood patterns that may later become adult problems.

The Basic Psychological Building Block

We learn who we are as human beings in relationships. We learn who we are. We learn who the other is and what the world is like. We learn what it feels like to be in those relationships and we learn a pattern of behavioral interchange with others. These principles, clear to any observer, have been explored in case histories uncovered during psychodynamic therapies and outlined in those object relations[47] and interpersonal theories derived from them. They have been operationalized, observed, and tested by developmental psychologists

---

[47] "Object relations" is an odd phrase. Derived from Freud's use of the term to denote that to which we emotionally connect, it was used to shift Freud's theory from a focus on the primacy of drives—sex and aggression—to the primacy of relationship in human motivation. Object relations theories and therapies are those that focus on the relationship of self and other within the psyche.

in work on attachment[48] and on social and emotional development[49]. The basic building block of personality is the experience of the growing infant in her earliest intimate relationships.

The Childhood Problem

The cards we are dealt as human beings include our genes, our unique environment including the generational context into which we are born, and the motivations that we have in common with all humans and all living beings. When we are born, we bring a set of potentialities into the world—those capacities that make us human as well as those that are unique to each of our individual selves. Perhaps we tend to a sensitive nervous system. We may be introverted or are extroverted. Perhaps we are particularly beautiful and graceful, or particularly intelligent in mechanics or mathematics. Perhaps we are especially coordinated or strong. Perhaps we are the opposite. There is a strong case for genetic predisposition for certain personality characteristics such as intelligence, openness, shyness, or introversion and extraversion, but even in these particularly strong cases, genes explain at most only half of the variance among individuals.

So, though genetic predisposition is important, environment or "nurture" is the deciding factor in forming our characters. We learn who we are as important people in our lives respond to us. Are we shy in a family of extroverts? Are we clumsy when our fathers were athletic, or did they too fail in sports? Are we so charming or sympathetic that we drew our mother's special attention and our father's jealous distance? Did a sibling with special needs require our parents' care while we were left on our own because we were

---

[48] Attachment theory, developed by psychoanalyst John Bowlby, has become a significant area of developmental research, beginning with the work of Mary Ainsworth and the so-called "Strange Situation."
[49] See, for example, Daniel N. Stern's *The Interpersonal World of the Infant,* Basic Books, 1985.

"normal"? Each of these and myriads of other combinations of infant characteristics and parental responses create sets of real circumstances to which the child must adapt in order to meet his or her basic human needs and thus to survive.

In addition to these givens—genetic predispositions and their environmental contexts—human beings are motivated to meet certain needs. Those needs are physical, of course, but also psychological, intellectual, social, and even spiritual. We experience these needs emotionally—as longings—and intensely—as hunger or thirst, whether it is a physical need for food or water, or the psychological need for connection and attachment. Though these needs are common to humankind, they can be specially reinforced by our particular early experiences. We long to be loved and close to another, to belong, to be truly known and understood, to be free to be ourselves, to learn and to explore and to grow, to make a difference in the world, to relate to something larger than ourselves. We are also motivated to make meaning of what we encounter, to understand why, and to develop theories to explain the world and ourselves.

In the same way, human beings are generally motivated to avoid pain, physically as well as psychologically. Pain is an early warning system that tells us our needs are not being met or our survival is threatened. We learn to fear what brings us pain, to try to avoid it. This is simply good sense. Like the association of need and longing, avoidance of pain is experienced emotionally as anxiety and fear. Many of our fears are also common to humankind, based on the existential realities all human beings confront. We fear physical pain and social ostracism. We fear death, isolation, meaninglessness, freedom, and even the responsibility to craft our lives that choice brings.[50] We fear

---

[50] See the seminal text, *Existential Psychotherapy,* by Irvin D. Yalom (HarperCollins Publishers, 1980).

emptiness, guilt, and condemnation.[51] But many of our fears—the ones we struggle with again and again—are fears learned from real experiences, especially with those we love or upon whom we depend. We fear that we will be rejected, used, intruded upon, criticized and condemned, abused, abandoned, invisible, misunderstood, found not good enough, left alone, and much more. We may learn these lessons in adulthood, but the most powerful and unconscious of our fears derive from our earliest experiences of relationship.

Childhood Solutions

Motivated by needs and fears, and in the real circumstances created by being *this* child with *this* parent or caretaker, we evolve our best solutions to the complex problems that present themselves, universally and also uniquely, in our earliest relationships. For example, we all experience being small and dependent in the care of powerful and independent adults. Was our mother nurturing and appropriately responsive, the "good enough mother,"[52] who let us explore and also cling according to our need, or was she depressed, or anxious, or needy, or controlling, or abusive, or rejecting, or intrusive? We learn both sides of our relationship to her: what it is to be vulnerable, needy, and dependent and what it is to be powerful and independent. Her individual response to our vulnerability teaches us what vulnerability means and also what power, responsibility, nurture, or independence means. Later, experience in relationship with our primary caretaker is elaborated as our circle of relationships grows. Finally, we use these very real experiences to develop theories about ourselves and others and the relationship between us.

---

[51] See Paul Tillich's brilliant work, *The Courage To Be* (Yale University Press, 1952).

[52] D.W. Winnicott, "Transitional Objects and Transitional Phenomena," *International Journal of Psychoanalysis* (34:89-97): 1953.

The solutions we devise to meet these problems are as varied as the problems themselves. We may learn to be quiet and invisible to avoid destructive envy. Like Sarah, we may learn to take care of our caretakers, to be organized and sensitive and responsible when they are not, or we may discover that the best defense is a good offense, attacking before we are attacked. We may find that a parent needs us to need them, teaching us to curtail our striving for independence, to become needy and full of self-doubt. We may become the clown or the black sheep or the hero. In our family, or in our role within that family, we may become insensitive or sensitive, caretaking or careless, responsible or irresponsible, leading or a following, guarded or boundary-less.

We learn these fundamental lessons early and often preverbally. Our earliest family relationships comprise our universe. So much so, in fact, that what we learn is largely unconscious. We simply assume it is so and must universally be so. We may codify these lessons in sayings or family rules or early memories, but for the most part they are simply unexamined assumptions. They comprise a set of deeply held beliefs about ourselves, others, and the world. They create a set of expectations about our relationships.

The Adult Problem

Having learned these powerful lessons, we go out into the world, operating on the basis of our beliefs and role expectations with those we meet and the situations we encounter. This is an elegant system meant to enable us to adapt, survive, and thrive in the larger world, but what if the larger world is not like the one in which we grew up? What if the other person is not like the ones we first knew? What if, in fact, *we* are not like what our loved ones taught us that we are? What if we do not fit the theories we ourselves have derived to explain why our loved ones react to us as they do? Then our early learning may not apply, and worse, may actually create problems for us. Joseph's bragging brought adoration from his parents, but fanned the flames of destructive envy in his big brothers. The Israelites flourishing as a separate people elicited fearful oppression in Egypt.

Three processes may contribute to those problems. First, we elicit the responses we expect through the behaviors we have learned. Second, we tend to select significant others based on deep emotional attractions or revulsions to what is learned and familiar, and third, we tend not to see new choices because our beliefs, conscious and unconscious, guide our perceptions.

First, like self-fulfilling prophecies, the behaviors based on our early beliefs actually create what we expect to find. We elicit in others the responses we expect them to have. If a child expects his mother to be angry, he may learn to hide unwelcome facts or feelings from her, avoiding the reaction he fears. As he grows, employing this strategy with others—perhaps his teacher or his friend—his avoidance itself and the repercussions of it may *make* them angry! If a child learns to fear exclusion by loved ones and to cope successfully with that fear by performing and prowess, she may later find that friends and lovers tire of her efforts to entertain, finally turning from her and excluding her just as she has always feared! We have seen how Joseph's efforts to secure his place as favorite son and to avoid the abandonment his family feared actually triggered that very abandonment.

Second, if early learning can create the familiar patterns of relationship, it also provides a template of familiarity that guides us in selecting those closest to us. We respond emotionally, in attraction or repulsion, to those who play a complementary role to our own. What is most intimately familiar feels like love. We hate and attack that which is most intimately feared. In a complex combination of both of these dynamics, couples are attracted to aspects of each other that may ultimately polarize their relationship. In therapy, they often find that their complementary roles and behaviors, initially attracting and ultimately frustrating, are rooted in similar early learning and identical conflicts.

Finally, the beliefs derived from these earliest experiences guide and also limit our choices in life. A wonderful illustration of this principle is the story of how a young elephant is trained. When he is a baby, he is tied to a stake in the ground so that he won't wander away. He can pull and pull, but he cannot pull that stake out. When he is a grown elephant he could pull the entire circus big top down and drag it through Main Street, but he doesn't. He doesn't believe he can. He has changed, but his beliefs about himself and the world have not. These beliefs guide and limit his perceptions and therefore his choices.

Sarah had learned early how to take care of her loved ones. In marriage, she had chosen a partner who needed and valued her care. Years later, she found she was an enabler to an alcoholic husband, subtly communicating to him that she did not expect him to be able to take care of himself, of her, of their children. Yet, despite being drunk every night, he was respected and capable each day in a demanding and responsible leadership position in a large company. He was actually a man able to wield power and take responsibility. Somehow her efforts and her expectations did not fit these facts, while at the same time they helped to create the very problems she would most wish to avoid. Now what could she do? To her, both confronting him and leaving him seemed equally unloving, uncaring, and untenable. Egypt.

In the same way that the children of Israel became slaves in Egypt, our early learning and the solutions we develop to cope with real problems guide, create, and limit the lives we live as adults. Sarah's journey has just begun. Let's consider another patient who found himself enslaved in a very similar way.

Susan Davis, Ph.D.

The Ideal Husband

Pete wrote this poem about the beginning of his therapy process:

Continuation

My first sense of clarity came from you
Who instigated the rage of love inside all other places
And made other storms distant and orbital
There is a sanctuary to the silence of intelligence
But how can I know anything at all
When my heart has no place to be known
Outside the savagery of its immense light?

"How can I know anything at all/When my heart has no place to be known?" Unhappy in his marriage and feeling used by his employees, Pete beautifully expressed his hunger to understand what caught him in his own personal Egypt. He describes the very human longing to be intimately known and to know, to be understood and to understand, which is so much what being loved and loving in return is all about.[53]

This becoming known is also what good psychotherapy is all about. Bringing our old learnings into conscious awareness to be re-evaluated is a large part of any psychotherapy. Therapist and client explore old history and current problems, dreams and desires, and their mutual experience of the therapeutic relationship itself to understand the learnings that have become beliefs, unconscious assumptions about the self and the other. Together they observe and question the client's beliefs about themselves, others, and the world.

[53] Paul Tournier's little book, *To Understand Each Other*, first brought this point home to me—(John Knox Press, Richmond, Virginia, 1973, published originally in French, 1962: Difficultes conjugales, Editions Labor et Fides, Geneva, Switzerland).

42

As this process unfolds, the client's beliefs and familiar roles will be enlarged, made more accurate, and finally made more flexible and adaptive. The experience of the therapeutic relationship offers the client a new template for beliefs, role expectations, and feelings about themselves and another, and in this way, an opportunity to craft a different world. That is what Pete and I were working to do together.

The Adult Problem

Good-looking, talented, and loving, Pete was the ideal husband. He worked hard to take care of his wife and children, and usually took the blame for any problem that arose between them. When he first came for therapy, he was developing his own high-tech start-up company while his wife stayed home with their two children. He would put in a long day at work and return home to help with the shopping, cooking, cleaning, washing up, gardening, and laundry. He was home three nights a week to care for his children while his wife attended classes that interested her. When he went to bed, he went alone while his wife stayed up late and then slept in the kids' room with their infant son. Up early, Pete left them sleeping and went out to drum up more funding and manage his staff. This pattern had persisted for over two years. Pete felt lonely and used by those he loved and even by some he employed—but why did he let them get away with it?

Childhood Problems and Solutions

When Pete was a child, his mother was frequently depressed, withdrawing into her room for days, leaving her children worried and lonely. Perhaps his parents' marriage was a source of pain for both of them, but whatever the cause, Pete's father was also stressed and unhappy. He took his frustration out physically and verbally on his children, often blaming Pete for causing his mother's depression. He was competitive with his sons, refusing to allow them to succeed in any way that made him feel unsuccessful.

Sensitive and gifted, Pete believed that he deserved his father's beatings. Many times our childhood beliefs are based on our universal efforts to see our parents as all-good, to protect them and to love them. If there is a problem, we attribute it to ourselves. Pete took the blame for his own loneliness, neglect, and physical abuse as a child. He tried to love and take care of his mother better, and he tried not to trigger his father's anger and abuse. He believed that if there was a problem, he was to blame. This was a brilliant coping strategy for a tenderhearted child with nowhere else to go.

But as an adult, this strategy had become a problem, his Egypt. His ways of thinking and feeling about himself and others had helped to create the frustrating and lonely world in which he now found himself. Like Sarah, being such a caring and care-taking person, he found himself surrounded by people who wanted that care. Taking the responsibility and the blame, he found himself surrounded by people who blamed him and would not take responsibility themselves. His old learnings did not fit the facts: though he actually was attractive and desirable, he did not see himself this way. Moreover, since he'd never experienced it, he did not expect relationships to be built on reciprocity and mutual respect. As a result, he surrounded himself with others whose responses to him fit his expectations and were familiar experiences. He selected a wife who, like his mother, was withdrawn and disengaged from him and who, like his father, was competitive, explosive, and demanding of him. He experienced panic at the idea of leaving her or of being left by her.

It was no surprise, then, that his relationships exhausted him, made him angry, then guilty and afraid, and left him feeling alienated and alone. Not risking failure, he was afraid to expect better, much less to let go the little he had. He had begun to have panic attacks. Interchanges with his wife were mostly avoidant with intermittent adversarial confrontations. His children were beginning to show the same competitive, explosive, and demanding behaviors as their mother.

Two years and many sessions later, Pete came to therapy glowing after a talk with his sister "about our Dad!" He had begun to know quite a lot about the old learnings that had shaped his inward and outer life. He said,

> "We never talk about what happened. But last night, she talked about his abuse of her, how she remembers being beaten with his belt when she was five years old and even being knocked unconscious when she was ten! She was beaten like me. My granddad was raised by *his* grandfather in the Philippines, and he remembered beatings, too. Five generations of fathers beating their kids. My sister said that she felt she had to be perfect to try to avoid those beatings, so she didn't try things she wasn't good at—like me! Remember how I told you I had such bad stage fright as a little kid in grade school? I didn't want to appear foolish. And in high school I was a really good basketball player, really talented. My coach suggested that since I'm left-handed, I develop my right hand so I could use both. I would have been great. But I didn't do it—I was afraid to fail. Even now, I don't try with women . . ."

Pete had begun to change. He had begun to understand his family patterns and the way his coping strategies were affecting his life. He had begun to wonder whether he might be worth something, whether he could set boundaries in relationships at home and at work, whether to hope for more from his life and his loved ones. He began to ask his wife for changes. Suddenly she said she wished to separate from him. It became clear that she had begun an affair. As Pete grappled with this new betrayal, struggling to work through his fears of abandonment, he slowly began to realize that divorce, for him, might be a blessing in disguise. For the Israelites, leaving Egypt—or even being thrown out—might be a good thing.

A few months later, he had this dream: *"I was in my house—someone was making me and others be there, and they were gonna blow it up! We were waiting to be killed . . . then I realized we could get out and go into the yard! When we got out into the yard, the house blew up, and then we feared they'd find us in the yard!"* It was a perfect picture of his experience of his divorce at that point in time—he'd gotten out into the yard. He realized he'd survived so far, but was still afraid of what might come as the couple settled issues of finance and custody. It was also a perfect picture of his inner growth in changing his early beliefs about himself and his loved ones. He had realized he could move outside of the old life and the old beliefs, though he still felt in peril of persecution and destruction as he abandoned his early learnings and loved ones by seeing things differently. But we are getting ahead of ourselves and anticipating a later stage in the Exodus story: leaving Egypt and crossing the Red Sea. Back to Egypt for now!

Safety, Slavery, and Compromise

Psychologist James Bibb, my mentor and director of training during my predoctoral internship at the Queen's Medical Center in Honolulu, taught that our lives are compromises between our longings and our fears. The safety that becomes slavery is such a compromise. Israel's family longed for security and survival in Egypt, but feared to be lost as a people in the shuffle of Egyptian society. Their compromise, to be separate by being disrespected, ultimately led to a very difficult problem to solve—slavery, and worse, a slave mentality. As we have seen, our very human longings and fears and the solutions we've evolved to cope with childhood problems set up the patterns of compromise that become our adult problems. When he began therapy, Pete's life and marriage was such a compromise.

The problem with compromises between our longings and our fears is that they don't actually satisfy our longings, and they can create the very fears they were meant to avoid. In the end, we are still left to face our fears and seek our longings. Thoreau spoke of it in this way:

> If the condition of things which we were made for is not yet, what were any reality which we can substitute? We will not be shipwrecked on a vain reality. Shall we with pains erect a heaven of blue glass over ourselves, though when it is done we shall be sure to gaze still at the true ethereal heaven far above as if the former were not?[54]

We may long for the clear blue of the true sky, but what if we are afraid of the rain or the wind or the darkness of night? Would a dome of blue glass satisfy us? The closed-off, walled-in space under that blue dome may become secure and familiar, but it would be a prison nonetheless. The compromises we make between our longings and our fears become our prisons.

Worse, compromised choices ultimately hurt us. The ancient Greeks told the story of travelers who stayed in a diabolical inn. At night they were made to fit the bed they laid down in; their bodies were stretched if they were too short, cut off if they were too tall. We think this is horrifying torture, and it is. Yet how many times do we find ourselves in the same situation, ourselves the innkeeper as well

---

[54] Henry David Thoreau, Walden; or, Life in the Woods (New York: Dover Publications, Inc., 1995), p. 211. First published by Ticknor & Fields, Boston, 1854.

as the guest? Like the traveler whose bones are stretched out or feet cut off to fit the bed, the lives we live from compromises between our longings and our fears result in physical and emotional pain for ourselves and/or for our loved ones. Unsatisfied longings and un-confronted fears cannot safely be contained in the human psyche. Instead, they leak out, manifesting in the diseases that lead us to doctors and counselors, the anger of a child, the loneliness of our spouse, the problems in our organizational cultures, the dysfunction of nations and ecosystems.

Pete's early poem continued in this way:

> I notice the reinventing landscape
> I notice the change in the rooms
> I notice time flowing out across those places
> While the whole of me turns around
> Hoping for something better out of the beginning.

Like the children of Israel, our dilemma is how to break out of the inner psychological slavery that has now become an external and real slavery as well. Our first step is to become aware of our childhood solutions to real problems and of the longings and fears that continue to compromise our lives. Then, like Pete, do we dare to hope for something better out of the beginning? Like the Israelites, do we dare to cry for deliverance? With my patient Joanna, do we dare ask: "Where is my internal Moses?"

The shadow that follows us is the way in.
Rumi

What you're after is truth from the inside out.
David

Chapter Four:
Where is My Internal Moses?

Moses. The life and personality of this man have left their indelible mark on two of the world's great religions, Judaism and Christianity, and through them on western culture itself. His vivid personality confronts us today as we read of events that took place between 1250 and 1300 B.C.[55], 3300 years ago. But what did Joanna mean when she asked, "Where is my internal Moses?" Let's begin to answer that question by meeting the man central to the Exodus story, the prophet like no other in Israel's history, "whom God knew face-to-face."[56]

Man of anger and impulse; murderer; champion of the oppressed; mystic and prophet; breaker of the tablets on which were written God's ten commandments—Moses was also stammering and self-doubting, begging God to "send someone else!"[57] Exodus tells us he

---

[55] *The Renovaré Spiritual Formation Bible,* NRSV, ed. Richard Foster (Harper San Francisco, 2005), p 93.
[56] Deuteronomy 34:10
[57] Exodus 4:13

was born a Hebrew in Egypt in the time we have just explored, when male babies were under edict of death because Egypt felt threatened by its healthy and flourishing Israelite population.

The Exodus Story

As the story is told, his mother hid him for three months until she could hide him no more. Then she put him in a basket in the bulrushes of the Nile, watched over by his sister.

> The baby's older sister found herself a vantage point a little way off and watched to see what would happen to him. Pharaoh's daughter came down to the Nile to bathe; her maidens strolled on the bank. She saw the basket-boat floating in the reeds and sent her maid to get it. She opened it and saw the child—a baby, crying! Her heart went out to him. She said, "This must be one of the Hebrew babies."

> Then his sister was before her: "Do you want me to go and get a nursing mother from the Hebrews so she can nurse the baby for you?" Pharaoh's daughter said, "Yes. Go." The girl went and called the child's mother. Pharaoh's daughter told her, "Take the baby and nurse him for me. I'll pay you."

> The woman took the child and nursed him. After the child was weaned, she presented him to Pharaoh's daughter who adopted him as her son. She named him Moses (meaning "Pulled-Out"), saying, "I pulled him out of the water."[58]

Raised in Pharaoh's court, a Hebrew among Egyptians, Moses was indeed "pulled out"—out of the river and out of his family and culture. It must have been a complicated childhood, but the Bible

---

[58] Exodus 2:4-10

simply says, "Time passed. Moses grew up."[59] The next bit in the narrative tells us that upon seeing an Egyptian overseer beating a Hebrew slave, and overwhelmed by fury at this and all the injustices and suffering Egypt was meting out to the Israelites, Moses killed the overseer and buried his body in the sand. Thinking he'd gotten off with no witnesses, he was shocked and terrified when he found his secret was known. Furthermore, Pharaoh, his adoptive grandfather, was seeking him to kill him. He panicked and ran.

Finding himself in Midian by a well, Moses again showed his gallantry and passion for the oppressed. He protected several women from the men who were harassing them at a well and lifted the heavy water jars to water their sheep. When offered hospitality by their father Jethro, priest of Midian, Moses stumbled onto a new world in which to live. He married Zipporah, one of Jethro's daughters, fathered a son, and became shepherd to Jethro's flocks. Pharaoh's daughter's Hebrew son, raised in the highest court of the most advanced civilization of his time, had found an uncomplicated life.

His story had just begun, however, and his life was about to become very complicated. Some years later, guiding the sheep in the western wilderness on the mountain called Horeb, Moses had a mystical experience. He encountered something strange: a bush that blazed with flame but did not burn.

He looked. The bush was blazing away, but it didn't burn up.
Moses said, "What's going on here? I can't believe this! Amazing! Why doesn't the bush burn up?"[60]

Then an even more amazing thing happened. As he approached, he heard the voice of God call his name. "Moses! Moses! . . . Don't come any closer. Remove your sandals from your feet. You're standing on

[59] Exodus 2:11
[60] Exodus 3:2-3

holy ground."[61] What a strange experience—something numinous, holy, and wholly other—and that Other knew his name.

Next, Moses and God had a most surprising, challenging, and history-altering conversation. It began as God told Moses that *he* was angry about the very thing *Moses* had been most angry about:

> God said, "I've taken a good, long look at the affliction of my people in Egypt. I've heard their cries for deliverance from their slave masters; I know all about their pain. And now I have come down to help them, pry them loose from the grip of Egypt, get them out of that country and bring them to a good land with wide-open spaces, a land lush with milk, and honey . . . . The Israelite cry for help has come to me, and I've seen for myself how cruelly they're being treated by the Egyptians. It's time for you to go back: I'm sending you to Pharaoh to bring my people, the people of Israel, out of Egypt."[62]

Though Moses agreed with God's cause, he did not agree with God's plan where he himself was concerned. Moses was afraid. He questioned, "Why me?"[63] He offered his objections: Why would anyone believe that you sent me? Who are you, anyway? I'm not a good motivational speaker! Send someone else! Moses argued with God. God answered his arguments, demonstrated miraculous power, and finally got angry with all Moses' equivocation and dilly-dallying. Then Moses was on his way back to Egypt with his family.

Next comes a very enigmatic and puzzling passage, one we will address again later in this chapter. After God's dramatic call and with Moses obedient to his command, it seems God now intended

---

[61] Exodus 3:4-5
[62] Exodus 3:7-10
[63] Exodus 3:11

to kill Moses! "On the journey back, as they camped for the night, God met Moses and would have killed him but Zipporah took a flint knife and cut off her son's foreskin, and touched Moses' member with it . . . . Then God let him go."[64]

What on earth is going on? Flaming bushes that do not burn, calls to do impossible and dangerous things, strange and bloody rituals? The story of the burning bush communicates the mysterious and life-changing, life-focusing wonder of an encounter with the divine. This is the realm of theology, but can psychology also offer something to help us understand this strange and fascinating story? Can it show us a way to encounter and make sense of those forces within ourselves that disturb and move us toward transformation? Let's consider the Jungian concept of the Shadow.

The Shadow

The great psychiatrist and founder of analytic psychology, Carl Jung, conceived of a powerful and useful theory of psychological development. Breaking away from his mentor Sigmund Freud, Jung explored his own dreams and fantasies as well as those of his patients.[65] His theory, in brief, is that we are born with undifferentiated but complete human potential—the Self with a capital S. That Self comprises all that belongs to our own unique genetic make-up as well as that which is common to all humanity. As we grow, we learn what is acceptable to our families and cultures, embracing those aspects of Self as "me," our conscious identity or self (with a small s). Those aspects of ourselves we deem unacceptable—our subjective experiences and our feelings—we reject as "not me"[66] and repress away from our conscious awareness. Then, instead of being "pulled

[64] Exodus 4:24-25
[65] See Jung's spiritual autobiography, *Memories, Dreams, Reflections*.
[66] For the usage of "me" and "not me" I am indebted to one of my mentors, the psychiatrist and Jungian analyst, Michael Horne, MD.

out," claimed and redeemed as Moses was, a part of our real Self is split off. In condemning certain actions or acting-outs, for example, we learn to reject the feelings associated with the behaviors—anger, desire, fear, sadness. In condemning certain feelings, we learn to divide aspects of ourselves from our conscious identities—power, leadership, awareness, creativity, compassion, sexuality. We lose touch with important aspects of ourselves, aspects we need in order to respond well in particular situations.

We come to reject aspects of ourselves by direct parental and societal teaching and by indirect but powerful painful experience. Trauma plays its part. So does the continual, repetitive cycle of the interpersonal patterns experienced in our earliest and most intimate relationships—as we have already discussed in chapter three. Those aspects of ourselves that do not fit in with our gender identity Jung called the anima (for men) and the animus (for women). That which we consider dangerous or evil Jung called the Shadow.

The Shadow, that part of ourselves we don't trust and don't want to know, pursues us nonetheless. It *is* we ourselves, and we are not complete, whole, without it. It leaks out in the ways we behave— as the apostle Paul writes of his own experience, "What I don't understand about myself is that I decide one way, but then I act another, doing things I absolutely despise."[67] A client once said, "I don't know who that bitch is driving down the freeway, but that is NOT ME!" Our Shadow speaks to us in psychological and physical symptoms through the body. It knows what we don't know, speaks the unspeakable about our loved ones and ourselves. It chases us in our most terrifying dreams as we run from killer whale or giant snake, young lion or grizzly bear, forest fire and tidal wave, bomb or burning bush, murderer, burrowing witch, monster. We are sure

---

[67] Romans 7:15

that if we are caught we will be killed or our world destroyed, and in a sense that is true.

The self we have cultivated and known, our conscious identity or ego, would be changed. The world we've built for ourselves, perhaps constricting but nonetheless familiar, may also be changed. Jung's idea of the Shadow is that as we encounter it, we are transformed, made whole, balanced and complete. In that sense it does destroy the old familiar self, but the Shadow itself is transformed by this encounter, brought home, and civilized. We need this wholeness, this growing toward the fullest expression of our true Self.

The poet E.E.Cummings describes it this way:

> a total stranger one black day
> knocked living the hell out of me—
>
> who found forgiveness hard because
> my (as it happened) self he was
>
> —but now that fiend and I are such
> immortal friends the other's each[68]

Cummings' play on words—that this stranger "knocked living the hell out of me"—suggests not just the shock of an encounter with our Shadows, but also the transformative power of that encounter. It's not just that the Shadow knocked the livings out of us, but it is the hell we are living that is knocked out of us. Then the poet underscores the deep intimacy of this encounter: "my (as it happened) self he was." The Shadow is that within us that we have disowned and buried alive, but can never be rid of because our (as it happens) self it is.

---

[68] E. E. Cummings, *A Selection of Poems*, (Harcourt Brace Jovanovich, New York and London), from *95 Poems*, written in 1958, p, 151.

Moses' Shadow and the Flame that Does Not Consume

Moses' Shadow was his anger, the righteous indignation ignited by oppression.[69] The bush that burned but was not consumed is a perfect symbol for his anger, his Shadow. Don't the words that came to Moses from the bush voice precisely his old sense of injustice and violation? "'The Israelite cry for help has come to me, and I've seen for myself how cruelly they're being treated by the Egyptians. It's time for you to go back: I'm sending you to Pharaoh to bring my people, the People of Israel, out of Egypt.'"[70] At that point, Moses had learned to suppress his sense of injustice and violation and his gallant urge to right what was wrong. In that suppression, he had lost an important aspect of himself—his passion, his power, and so his courage. Perhaps we could understand that process better by looking at the foundation of his character and his distrust in anger and power.

In Moses' earliest years, there must have been many messages urging him to be quiet, unassuming. Hushed by his mother in the cradle, hidden for three months—her message was, "Moses! Don't cry out! Your life depends on it!" As the child grew to manhood in the Egyptian court, perhaps the message of his princess mother was: "Moses, be careful! The court is a dangerous place. People seek advantage. Don't reveal yourself to them—don't be open and vulnerable! People will exploit your weakness, your passion. Hide it!"

---

[69] My thoughts on this point were stimulated by a seminar, "Men and Anger," led by Stephen C. Simmer, LICSW, Ph.D., I attended on 7/21/2001. Dr. Simmer used Shinto imagery to describe the integration of the Shadow: anger as a daemon in the form of a dragon that must be contained in a vessel so that it may be transformed into a noble, wise, human presence, an inner teacher giving voice to one's values and a drive for justice.

[70] Exodus 3:9-10

Growing up at court, a Hebrew among Egyptians, an adoptive son not born in his mother's household, he must have experienced rejection, subtle and perhaps not so subtle. He must have seen arrogance and prejudice and oppression. Wouldn't a passionate anger be our natural human reaction to any of this? Anger motivates us to do what needs to be done. Yet it may be dangerous to do what we think needs to be done. It may be dangerous to express that anger. Anger expressed, change sought, boundaries set might spark more rejection or even retaliation. So we tell ourselves, "Don't rock the boat; don't stick your neck out; put up and shut up; keep your head down." We repress that anger—survival is at stake. We push it down, sometimes so deep that we don't consciously recognize it anymore.

Moses must surely have experienced this kind of anger. Yet as we have imagined it, the teaching of both his mothers would have reinforced a damping down of his justifiable anger, his righteous indignation. The social and political realities of Egyptian society at that time in history would have taught him it was not safe to express it. He must have felt, as we might feel, oppressed, judged, rejected, used, ridiculed, and even abused—and resentful of it. Conflicted over his anger, Moses might have found himself guilty and afraid of it, but impotent and afraid without it.

Yet what is repressed is not inert. It leaks out, sometimes explodes like a pressure cooker heated with no safety valve, no steam release. For Moses, that explosion came when he saw the Egyptian overseer beating a Hebrew slave, his countryman. He became a murderer. Fleeing for his life, the lesson was reinforced: it is dangerous to let your anger out! Then Moses' efforts to hide or get rid of his Shadow would have been redoubled. When we meet the shepherd Moses years later, we see someone different from the passionate young courtier who killed a vicious overseer, different from the gallant young man who rescued Jethro's daughters. This Moses is a man who feels insecure, who doesn't trust himself, who feels weak and ineffective. He has accomplished the splitting off of his passion, but at a price. In losing this aspect of himself, he has lost some part of his virility, his masculine power, his daring and his confidence. We, too, are diminished by repression, by the fear of our feelings and the rejection of ourselves that we now—no longer needing anyone else's help—accomplish on our own. We cease to be the whole, vital, alive people we long to be and that God intended us to be.

Let's turn from Moses for a moment and consider my patient, Sylvie, struggling with her Shadow in our more modern times.

The Brown Lump

Of Hispanic and French parentage, Sylvie was beautiful with her curly dark hair, almond brown eyes, and warm cappuccino-colored skin. Intense, intelligent, and insightful, she was finishing her master's degree in counseling despite the demands of work and young children. In our work together, she complained of her constant barrage of self-critical thoughts and nearly constant state of exhaustion and desire to sleep. "I just can't handle life! I feel bad, and I don't get better! I feel exposed without the façade of confidence I used to have. I feel like a failure in every area of my life. I feel vulnerable and I'm scared to exist!" She found herself paralyzed in making decisions, unable to prioritize all the things she should do, unsure of what she most wanted to do, tormented by doubt and insecurity in all she did do.

Over the years, she had struggled with the therapy process many times, even as she explored it in her counseling program. She wished for mastery and resisted any approach that made her feel small, vulnerable, and out of control. She preferred cognitive or behavioral or medical approaches that offered direct intervention with symptoms or, at the least, clear direction in what she should do.

Although we'd spoken of dreams and the therapeutic relationship, she had particularly resisted any approach using guided imagery and active imagination—until one interesting session. We began by focusing on the bodily sensations she experienced as she discussed her hopeless feelings. I prompted, "What do you notice in your body? Don't try to change it, just notice it for a moment."

"I feel nausea, my throat closing . . . a tight chest and throat . . . tears."

"Now shift your focus to your mind's eye," I suggested. "Is there a memory or picture, a word or sound, or anything you notice there?"

"Overwhelmed . . . like darkness is pushing in, expanding as I breathe in and getting smaller as I breathe out. Like a cloud or veil or something."

"Just watch for a moment. Is there anything else you notice?"

"You seem far away and going out and further away!" she said, her voice rising a little. "I'm alone. I'm a lump sitting here . . . a brown mass with a head! It's hard to stay with it. I could never do this as a therapist—I'm not skilled enough. The brown lump has *teeth*! It could swallow me up! This is bullshit."

"What is it like in your body now?"

"I'm not as nauseated, though I have a stomachache. You're closer."

"Okay," I said. "Let's come back to this moment here together and think about this."

As we began to consider this brief chain of unconscious material, we noticed an inner conflict. First there was the powerful intervention of her inner critical voice, "the strict side of me." That is the voice we heard when Sylvie said, "I could never do this as a therapist—I'm not skilled enough," and "This is bullshit." As we talked, she went on to describe the strict side: "It says: 'Cope! Stop being depressed!' I'm really just lazy."

The target of this bitter criticism was another aspect of herself, that "lump sitting here . . . a brown mass with a head!" Called "depressed, lazy, fat," the brown lump was hated and feared by the strict side. "The brown lump has *teeth!* It could swallow me up!" She feared that she could be absorbed by the lump and lost to it. During this exercise, Sylvie experienced the brown lump as nausea and a sense of overwhelm and tremendous aloneness. Its teeth suggest both need and anger—need and anger that Sylvie feared could swallow her up! Almost immediately the strict side stepped in to protect her with its driving criticism and mental toughness: "I could never do this. This is bullshit!" The strict side intervened to protect Sylvie from the possibility that the lump could swallow her up, that she could be lost in her feelings.

The strict side and the lump were locked in a battle to control Sylvie's life. She consciously identified with the strict side, but found herself again and again overpowered by the choices of the brown lump. How could the brown lump, Sylvie's rejected and hated Shadow, have any value whatsoever?

For years, Sylvie had sought some trauma in her history to explain her anxiety and depression. Had she been molested? Abused? No memories supported this hypothesis, but Sylvie's parents' marriage was an unhappy one. Her mother was close to her older son, but, angry and depressed, she had little to spare for a small curly-haired daughter. Her warm and charming father had struggled with a bipolar mood disorder that made his attention unreliable and intermittent. Sylvie's childhood pain was not the devastating blow of trauma, but the slow drop-by-drop water torture of emotional neglect. The strict side had developed to raise the child up by her bootstraps, to push her forward and guide her in the chaos and aloneness of her childhood.

Lost in that brilliant childhood adaptation were the genuine physical and emotional needs of the child. Those needs and feelings were worse than useless, they were actively destructive to a child raising herself—like a lump with teeth that could chew you up and swallow you. So she had repressed her awareness of them, attacking and criticizing them when they leaked out in physical and emotional symptoms.

Sometimes with patients like this I am reminded of the small, sturdy grey donkeys I saw in Greece. With their little round bellies, you could see them craning their necks to snatch a mouthful of purple thistles as they trudged along the road, driven by their masters. Loaded with packs or people, their drivers sweating in the summer sun, how they must have longed to roll in the grass or rest in the shade. If the driver were harsh and cruel, jerking the donkey's mouth away from the thistles, forcing her to go another mile without a drink of water, would he find himself beating an animal that lay down in the road regardless of the blows? If, on the other hand, he were kind and thoughtful, giving her rest and time to graze, would she serve him with willingness and renewed energy?

The brown lump is the little donkey, Sylvie's Shadow. The lump, Sylvie's physical and emotional need, continued to press for recognition, but she feared it with the child's survival panic. What might Sylvie's Shadow bring her? Overwhelm, helplessness, abandonment, panic? Or might it bring a mouthful of thistles, rest in the shade at high noon, an easier yoke and lighter burden, still waters, green pastures? It's interesting to notice that Sylvie ended the guided imagination exercise feeling better, less nauseated, more relaxed and connected to me. Perhaps Sylvie was just relieved that the exercise was over, or perhaps even this brief contact with a rejected part of herself eased an inner panic and misery.

We might consider the brown lump as the voice of God from the burning bush, the light of God from the depths of her Shadow. When she repressed awareness of her Shadow, Sylvie found herself paralyzed, sleeping, depressed, self-doubting. As she begins to listen within and to meet the needs she hears there—bit by bit, balancing them with what she ought to and must do in a fluid give and take—she will find that she is accomplishing even more in a day than she used to, has better ideas, and is more able to be present with her children, her husband, and her clients. She will be in touch with her priorities, able to make decisions because she would know what she wants to do, not just what she ought to do. She will feel more whole, more grounded, and more at peace.

The Shadow, the Holy, and Wholeness

As Sylvie's description of the brown lump hints, there is often a violent, off-putting quality to the presentation of the Shadow—E. E. Cummings captures this quality in his poem when he describes the other as "that fiend." The patient who declared she was not that "bitch driving down the freeway"—I'll call her Anne—later had a dream in which she was raped by a man who thought her weak and vulnerable. This dream figure was her Shadow, her repressed anger and capacity for assertiveness. The Shadow often presents in dreams or images of sex and violence that feel frightening or shameful, primitive and dark. Sometimes it shows us pictures of open wounds or corpses, diagnosing us in graphic imagery. Still later Anne had a disturbing dream in which she was looking at a horrible, deep wound in the back of her own neck. Her unconscious was showing her the psychological wound that cut her head off from her body, her conscious awareness from her physical and emotional experience.

Perhaps this frighteningly savage quality of the Shadow may help us understand the enigmatic passage in which it seemed God intended to kill Moses before Zipporah performed her strange circumcision ritual. As you recall, while camping for the night on the way to Egypt, "God met Moses and would have killed him."[71] Then, his wife took a flint knife and cut off their son's foreskin. She touched Moses' genitals with it, marking them with blood. As in Anne's dreams, there is sexuality, violence, and blood within this ritual. It is primitive, dark, unleashed, and disturbing.

This is exactly the way we experience an encounter with the Shadow. Sometimes it takes the bizarre and dramatic to get our attention, to focus and motivate us for the difficult tasks to which we are being called. Moses met the God of Abraham, Isaac, and Jacob when he approached the burning bush. That God spoke to him through the voice of his Shadow, the passion we are imagining he had repressed for so many years. There Moses confronted his own rage at injustice, aflame and searing with potentially destructive power, and he was afraid. We, too, are afraid. We believe that we will be killed by an encounter with the Shadow. In dreams, we run for our lives from monsters and murderers, from terrifying heights and the black abyss. We fall and drown and burn and die. Yet God's healing power is behind the Shadow from which we run.

On his way to Egypt, after his confrontation with the burning bush, Moses must have been struggling to understand and adapt to the life-changing encounter he had had. Old stirrings of that repressed young courtier must have disturbed his settled sense of himself as a simple shepherd. Memories of his own murderous rage must have threatened his sense of himself as a loving and nurturing son,

---

[71] Exodus 4:24

63

husband, and father. Doubts about his encounter with God and his revolutionary call to rescue Israel must have continued to haunt him. Using her feminine power as wife and mother, and the tradition of circumcision God had sanctified with Abraham to mark their special relationship, Zipporah created a ritual to help Moses integrate his own angry Shadow and to establish a new wholeness and sense of identity. He had lost the power and passion that gave virility and daring to his sensitivity and compassion, leaving him stammering and self-doubting. Her ritual brought together the split-off and disparate elements of Moses' psyche—the male power expressed in both his sexuality and his rage at oppression with the tender fathering nurture he felt toward his flocks and his small son. Her ritual also renewed the special identity of Moses and his people as chosen by God, connecting father and son in a generational line. Her ritual served as midwife to the changes conceived in Moses when he encountered God in the desert that day.

In a sense, Moses, the old Moses and his old ways of being either Shadow-run or running from his Shadow, did have to die for the new man and the new leader to emerge. The healing transformation God offers us is one designed to bring us back to a whole and integrated Self. Moses' integration gave the Israelites a prophet like no other, one with the courage and power to shepherd them on a journey of freedom, faith, and transformation.

Listening Within

What then is the path toward integration and wholeness? What is the alternative to splitting off aspects of ourselves, losing our power, when it leaks out anyway? The answer to the question, "Where is my internal Moses?" is both very simple and very difficult. We can listen within.

Listen within to our bodily and emotional feelings. We are often told that we should close down our feelings and not open them up; we should ignore them and not listen. Sometimes this comes from confounding feelings with actions, then applying moral condemnation to the feelings because the actions that might be inspired by them are destructive. Sometimes it comes from cultural values saying that there is no reality other than the material and external world—materialism and empiricism—or from the idea that conscious control of our thoughts is all that is necessary—cognitive approaches to psychology and faith. Sometimes we are so frightened of knowing ourselves and our feelings that we have cultivated manic approaches to life—get busy and run!—that are rewarded by our families and our society.

King David was known as a man after God's own heart. If you read his poetry, the book of Psalms, you meet a man who poured out his heart before God, a passionate man who acknowledged his genuine feelings to God. His psalms are full of frustration, resentment, confusion, and desire, as well as faith, joy, gratitude, awe, and love. Powerful in battle yet poetic in sensibility, David's great sin was his impulsive adultery with Bathsheba and then his intentional effort to cover it up by manslaughter.[72] Was this the result of a certain leaking out of inner feelings, this time unacknowledged and unrecognized? We know that he stood on his palace battlements at a time when kings went to war—yet this great warrior and general was not going to war with his troops. Perhaps this was David's midlife crisis, his facing of his own aging and mortality. After the prophet Nathan confronted him with his sin, as he reflected and returned to God, David sang, "You desire truth in the inward being. Therefore teach me wisdom in my secret heart."[73] Eugene Peterson translates it this way: "What you're after is truth from the inside out."

---

[72] See II Samuel 11 for this story.
[73] Psalm 51:6, NRSV

Listen within to the thoughts that run through our minds, barely perceptible and sometimes troubling and inconvenient. Elijah, second only to Moses as great prophet of Israel, found himself in trouble. Queen Jezebel was seeking his life, and he ran. He was exhausted and sick of the struggle, tired of doing the right thing only to be persecuted. He wanted to die. He walked to Mount Horeb, and sat down to listen to what God might say. There was a hurricane, an earthquake, and fire—but God was not in any of these cataclysms. Then, Elijah heard "a gentle and quiet whisper,"[74] or, as older translations have it, "a still, small voice."[75] That voice considered Elijah's exhaustion and depression with compassion and practical common sense. God advised: "Anoint Elisha son of Shaphat from Abel Meholah to succeed you as prophet."[76] Elisha became Elijah's companion and disciple for the remainder of his ministry, and later continued his prophetic work.

Moses' and Elijah's stories and David's poetry suggest that God's voice can be heard when we listen. Truth from the inside out, a still small voice or quiet whisper, a voice from the burning bush; what might we discover if we listen within ourselves? If we can bring our true feelings, our reactions, into the light of awareness and out of the shadows, might they be the voice of God calling us out of Egypt? Listen first, then reflect and decide what to do.

These three great men show us how to listen within ourselves—to bodily and emotional feelings, to inner thoughts, to parts of ourselves we fear and reject—in very practical ways.

---

[74] I Kings 19:12
[75] Revised Standard Version
[76] I Kings 19:16

David was confronted by the prophet Nathan.
> Listen to those you respect and trust. Find a good therapist or spiritual director. Consider what your children, spouse, parents, or siblings have to say.

David wrote his psalms.
> Journal—write freely without editing, hiding, judging. Paint, sculpt, dance, play music, cook, design, build.

Elijah went away.
> Retreat for a time. Go on vacation. Rest.

Moses approached the burning bush.
> Go toward that which you fear. Be curious about behaviors, dreams, symptoms, and odd thoughts.

The Balance that Makes Us Whole

The Shadow offers the balance that makes us whole. A dream, a crush, an obsession, a character flaw, even a sin can carry messages. We can notice, then reflect. This is how we begin the process of transformative change. Moses' encounter with the burning bush, though frightening and unwelcome, brought him power, courage, a sense of direction and a calling to do something—not impulsively and destructively, but intentionally and constructively.

For others that corrective balance might come in different ways. For some it is an awareness of vulnerability and need that fuels empathy for others and nurture for themselves. For some it is an awareness of a truth that brings clarity and freedom. For some it is a capacity for sensual pleasure that opens joy in the body and the created world. It could be love for something or someone that brings us out of our lonely autonomy—or the self-love of survival and healthy entitlement that brings us out of a hurtful relationship. Sometimes it is a restlessness or hunger for that which is unknown and beyond ourselves that leads us toward God.

Rumi, a thirteenth century Persian mystic, wrote:

> That which haunts us will find a way out.
> The wound will not heal unless given witness.
> The shadow that follows us is the way in.[77]

Where is my internal Moses? Moses was the baby found in among the river reeds who's name means "pulled out," like a baby pulled out of the bathwater. Our internal Moses—that part of ourselves with the courage to approach the burning bush and the capability to step out on a journey toward freedom and wholeness—is the baby in the bathwater. Listening within, we may hear the voice of God in those disowned feelings and aspects of ourselves Jung called the Shadow: the bitch driving down the freeway, Sylvie's brown lump, or Moses' burning bush. Becoming aware, reflecting, then choosing constructive action can begin to lead us out of a security that has become slavery and toward our Promised Land. With a very Jungian awareness, E. E. Cummings juxtaposed the words "fiend" and "friend" in the last couplet of his poem. He is describing the result of an encounter with the Shadow and the goal of the transformative journey: an integration in which the two aspects of ourselves become one. "The other's each."

If that is not enough, the very circumstances and outcomes we most dread and wish to avoid can also move us down the road to transformation.

---

[77] Rumi was born in 1207 and died in 1273. He was sheikh, religious scholar, and leader of the dervish learning community in Konya, Turkey. Unfortunately, I have lost track of this reference, but for his poems, see Coleman Barks' translation in *The Essential Rumi* (San Francisco, HarperCollins Publishers, 2004).

A mercy as severe as death, a severity as merciful as love.
Sheldon Vanauken

Chapter Five:
Homeostasis and Plagues

What do tiger sharks[78] along the coast of western Australian, sea otters in Monterey Bay, wolves in Yellowstone National Park, the Israelites in ancient Egypt, and each of us have in common? All are keystone species, playing a crucial role in a living system. A keystone species is a part of a community that, if removed from the system, changes the whole. Sea otters eat the sea urchins that feed on kelp, enabling a large number of fishes and other sea creatures to thrive in the great kelp forests along the west coast of the United States. Wolves influence elk behavior; tiger sharks influence the sea turtles and dugongs (Australian manatees) that graze the sea grasses. In turn, hundreds of other species of plants and animals are enabled to thrive.

For this reason, nature has evolved a complex set of finely tuned feedback loops to prevent change in a living system, something known as "homeostasis." Change is potentially destructive. Without otters, sea urchins proliferate, causing the kelp forests to die along with many of the fishes, invertebrates, and plants that they shelter

---

[78] Greg Laslo, "Predators as Key Players: How Sharks Shape the Marine Environment," *Dive Training*, (November 2006): 50-60.

and sustain. Without wolves or tiger sharks, whole ecosystems are in peril. Since change cascades through the entire system once it begins, in the natural course of things, change is not an easy thing to initiate.

However, when it's transformation we're after, change is exactly what we need. In Moses' time, change in the social, political, economic, and even psychological systems of both Egypt and Israel was desperately needed. Later in this chapter, we'll explore what psychology has discovered about changing psychological and social systems. Then we'll walk with a young couple in the midst of such change. First, let's explore what the Exodus story teaches us about how change was instigated in the ancient Egyptian-Israelite system.

The Exodus Story

After his encounter with the burning bush, Moses met his older brother Aaron in the desert wilderness of the Sinai to share the vision and mission God had given him. Together the brothers went to the leaders of the Israelites: "and the people trusted and listened believingly that God was concerned with what was going on with the Israelites and knew all about their affliction."[79] Then they went to Pharaoh with a slightly-less-than-honest request.

"God, the God of Israel, says, 'Free my people so that they can hold a festival for me in the wilderness.'"

Pharaoh said, "And who is God that I should listen to him and send Israel off? I know nothing of this so-called 'God' and I'm certainly not going to send Israel off."[80]

79 Exodus 4:31
80 Exodus 5:1-2

Pharaoh's response: assert homeostasis. Thus began a game of chicken between Pharaoh and Moses, between the status quo and liberating change. Pharaoh countered Moses, as do all systems, in a move designed to prevent further agitation for change. His second response to Moses' request was to prevent change by doubling the harsh workload of the Israelites until "they were beaten down in spirit by the harsh slave conditions."[81] In such a condition, how could the Israelites rebel against the system? They plummeted from hope to fear, rejoicing to misery—it wasn't going well.

> Then God said, "I am God. I appeared to Abraham, Isaac, and Jacob as The Strong God, but by my name (I-Am-Present) I was not known to them . . . I'll bring you into the land that I promised to give Abraham, Isaac, and Jacob and give it to you as your own country. I AM God."[82]

At this juncture of misery and clinging to the miserable but familiar, God revealed himself to Israel in a new way. Known as "the Strong God"—now God would be known as "I-Am-Present." And the strange and counter-intuitive way God chose to be present with them, according to the Exodus story, was to send an escalating and apocalyptic series of plagues.

First, the Nile was turned to blood so that the fish died. Then frogs overran the country, but Pharaoh's magicians could do the same tricks, so Pharaoh scoffed and refused to let Israel go. Next, "all the dust of the Earth turned into gnats, gnats everywhere in Egypt."[83] This was something the magicians could *not* do, but still Pharaoh refused. So flies covered Egypt—next livestock fell to disease and died—and then boils erupted on everyone. In the seventh plague, thunder, lightening, and hail ruined everything in the fields:

---

[81] Exodus 6:9
[82] Exodus 6:3, 8
[83] Exodus 8:17

humans, animals, plants, and trees. Still Pharaoh equivocated. An east wind blew clouds of locusts to eat every green thing that the hail had left. When Pharaoh still refused to let Israel go, "thick darkness descended on the land of Egypt for three days. Nobody . could see anybody. For three days no one could so much as move."[84] This I-Am-Present God continued to escalate plagues in order to accomplish change, but the Egyptian system was firmly rooted in homeostasis. Pharaoh refused.

Interestingly, the story suggests that the Israelites were specifically exempted from only half of these plagues: no flies, no dying animals, no hail, no darkness. Yet they witnessed and perhaps experienced the others: the Nile turning to blood, the frogs, gnats, locust, and boils. They must have been awestruck—and not in a nice way. They must have been at the least uncomfortable and more likely frightened as water became blood, fish died, frogs were everywhere, gnats swarmed. They may have been glad, but perhaps also nervous as Egyptian work bosses and wealthy aristocrats were struck down. They may have grieved Egyptian friends and neighbors. What an unwelcome kind of I-Am-Present was this! What sort of violent and terrifyingly primitive volcano god[85] had they invoked? What would

---

[84] Exodus 9:23

[85] Freud was fascinated and disturbed by the character of Moses. In his book, *Moses and Monotheism*, first published in 1939, he struggles to disengage from his own religious roots and to explain the development of monotheism in psychoanalytic terms: the guilt engendered by a hypothesized ancient patricide. He speculates that Moses was a composite figure: an Egyptian general and a Midianite shepherd. He suggests that Moses' God was also composite: a combination of the Egyptian monotheistic god Aton, the sun god, and the Midianite volcano god, Jahve. He notes the shaky ground on which his arguments are built in an early footnote: "When I use biblical tradition here in such an autocratic and arbitrary way, draw on it for confirmation whenever it is convenient, and dismiss its evidence without scruple when it contradicts my conclusions, I know full well that I am exposing myself to severe criticism concerning my method and that I weaken the force of my proofs." (New York: Random House, Vintage Books, p. 30) Yet he soldiers on, revealing less about Moses and monotheism, perhaps, than about his own inner conflicts with them.

happen next? Repeatedly, God explains that all of this is "so that you'll all know that I am God."[86]

Finally, the system began to crack open. Pharaoh began bargaining with Moses, "Okay, take your children, but leave your animals behind." Moses said no way. Pharaoh was caught in a face-losing situation, and he was angry.

> Pharaoh said to Moses: "Get out of my sight! And watch your step. I don't want to ever see you again. If I lay eyes on you again, you're dead."
>
> Moses said, "Have it your way. You won't see my face again."[87]

Then Moses confronted Pharaoh with a final warning: every firstborn among the Egyptians, human or animal, would die at midnight. With that, "Moses, seething with anger, left Pharaoh."[88] Here we see Moses, his passion and his Shadow power unleashed in the service of this great task.

God prepared to loose the tenth and final plague on Egypt as he issued instructions that would be commemorated in the Jewish holy day of Passover. Lamb's blood on the doorposts meant the angel of death would pass over that house. A meal of unleavened bread, bitter herbs, and a roasted lamb was to be eaten in a hurry, "fully dressed with your sandals on and your stick in your hand."[89] It was to be the final act in the escalating drama God had directed to disrupt the homeostatic system of ancient Egypt.

---

[86] Exodus 10:2; see also Exodus 8:22 and 9:14.
[87] Exodus 10:28-29
[88] Exodus 11:8
[89] Exodus 12:11

At midnight God struck every firstborn in the land of Egypt, from the firstborn of Pharaoh, who sits on his throne, right down to the firstborn of the prisoner locked up in jail. Also the firstborn of the animals.

Pharaoh got up that night, he and all his servants and everyone else in Egypt—what wild wailing and lament in Egypt! There wasn't a house in which someone wasn't dead.

Pharaoh called in Moses and Aaron that very night and said, "Get out of here and be done with you—you and your Israelites! Go worship God on your own terms. And yes, take your sheep and cattle as you've insisted, but go. And bless me."[90]

In a rush, the people of Israel began their journey out of Egypt. They took the gold and silver they'd been given by neighbors, their bread bowls filled with unrisen dough, their families and livestock: 600,000 Israelites with "a crowd of riffraff tagging along."[91] Egyptian homeostasis had been destabilized and cracked open by the plagues. The people of Israel were on the move.

Homeostasis and Change

In the early days of psychology, as we have seen, psychoanalysts and psychotherapists focused primarily on the individual who wanted or needed to change, but by the 1960's the new field of family systems therapy was taking hold as innovative researchers and therapists began to help individuals change by changing families. Like coral reefs or sea grass beds, the family came to be seen as an interconnected

---

[90] Exodus 12:29-32
[91] Exodus 12:38

system.[92] Individuals could change their families and families could change their individual members because systems are nested within and interconnected to each other. We have systems and systems of systems. This means that change at one level or in one system can trigger change in others, upward and downward, backward and forward throughout the network. The molecular connects to the physiological connects to the psychological connects to the social connects to the political, and so on and so on.

Systems are themselves living organisms and so seek to preserve themselves, to survive. To do so they must maintain internal stability—homeostasis—and so tend to resist change. We see this easily in ecosystems that can remain stable for thousands of years. Human systems are self-sustaining too, whether at the level of the individual's internal psychic structure, of a couple's unique relationship pattern, or of family or organizational culture. This becomes a problem if healing change is what we want. One of my favorite jokes—and probably the only one I can remember and tell reliably—highlights our difficulty: How many therapists does it take to change a light bulb? Only one—but the light bulb has to really want to change! Wanting to change—against the powerful forces of homeostasis—is tough to sustain, as anyone who has tried to diet, correct a tennis serve, or change a relationship pattern knows. Like the kelp forests along the Pacific coast or the Egypt of the Exodus account, systems resist change unless they experience some sort of dramatic, usually unwelcome, and sometimes terrifying intervention.

---

[92] Ludwig von Bertalanffy first proposed a general systems theory in the late 1920s, a theory which has come to influence biology, sociology and political science, economics, medicine, and philosophy, as well as psychology. He, along with Gregory Bateson, Margaret Mead, and other participants at the Macy conferences in the 1950s, developed a comprehensive theory that could be applied to all living systems, focusing on the interrelationships among parts of a whole instead of on the individual parts themselves.

The thermostat is a good metaphor for the mechanism by which an inner balance, homeostasis, is kept in systems. If the temperature gets too hot or too cold, moving outside certain set parameters, the thermostat activates or deactivates a furnace or air conditioner. This feedback loop serves to maintain homeostasis—in this case, an evenly balanced temperature. In the same way, natural ecosystems like reefs and forests—under normal conditions—use feedback loops such as the scarcity of food or excess of predators to maintain an exquisite balance. Like tyrants today, Pharaoh used the political power of oppression and repression to maintain a social, political, and economic system.

To understand how relational and psychological feedback loops maintain homeostasis, it is helpful to consider two interlocking levels of human systems: the intrapsychic and the interpersonal. The internal intrapsychic system is comprised of inner parts of the Self in relationship with each other. It is based on early learning about self and other in relationship, and in that sense begins as an internalized interpersonal system. Then it plays out in the world as we have seen. In previous chapters we used examples of the intrapsychic system when we discussed killer whales and the Susan in my dream, Jung's Shadow and the self, or conscious identity, Sylvie's brown lump and the strict side. The external interpersonal system is easier to see. It is formed by human beings in relationship: couples, families both nuclear and across generations, organizations, communities, cultures, countries.

In both types of systems, human emotions initiate the behaviors that maintain homeostasis. At the intrapsychic level, we experience guilt and anxiety when we deviate from internal standards of behavior. These are those standards, ways of being, we've been taught by family and culture or learned by early experiences. Interestingly, we feel the same guilt and anxiety whether aspects of those internal standards are flawed and unhelpful or not. In our interpersonal relationships, we experience longing and fear and anger—and others might exacerbate those feelings directly or indirectly. "I'm your mother!" or "I'll leave you!" or "I'm sick, come back!" or "Who do you think you are?" Perhaps they cry out, "You are so selfish!" or "I love you!" or "But you used to . . . !" Some threaten to commit suicide, some try to turn our children against us, some try to take us down financially or professionally. Fear, longing, anger, guilt, and anxiety are among the feelings that maintain intrapsychic and interpersonal homeostasis.

Among those feelings, fear of the unknown, guilt over changing what we've always learned, confusion as we doubt what we've always thought—these cannot be underestimated. Perhaps chief among these is fear—or its near cousin, anxiety—so let's focus on fear for a moment. Fear of change and of the unknown underlay the resistance of the Egyptians to let the Israelites go. Fear also plagued the Israelites in going, as we will see. Perhaps that is why God's plagues needed to be so frightening: the plagues and the people's sense of the awe-full power of God needed to be scarier than the alternative, the very scary unknown!

In our dreams, we play out this fear of the unknown and of transformative change in creative and dramatic format. We may see ourselves—the so-called "dream ego"—trying to bolt the windows against an intruder or running from danger and death. In Pete's dream, his house was being blown up; in mine, breeding killer whales would destroy humankind. In Sylvie's therapy exercise, the brown lump could swallow her whole. The Jungian analyst Michael Horne, M.D., once suggested that every transformation requires a death, the death of a world or of a way of being in the world.[93] For this reason, family therapists say that systems hate change. Change is painful, scary, threatening—even if the system is painful, even

---

[93] Personal Communication.

if the system exacts an intolerable price for participating in it. We prefer homeostasis unless the Shadow within or plagues without—or sometimes both—force us forward.

We have seen how the plagues disturbed the homeostasis of Egypt and so offered an opportunity for transformative change to both Egypt and Israel. Let's continue to explore examples of this process: first, by focusing on the intrapsychic experience depicted in a work of fiction and, second, by considering two very real people and the interpersonal systems within which they were embedded.

Changing Within

C.S. Lewis in his book, *The Great Divorce*, dramatizes the problem of internal change. Eventually, in almost every therapy, I find myself mentioning this wonderful, though relatively unknown, little book—which is not about the kind of divorce most of us expect it to be from the title. It's about the divorce between heaven and hell, about how the real choices we each make in life lead us along two radically diverging paths. In this imaginative work, the ghosts of the damned are given excursions to heaven. Once there, they are met by other souls who try to convince them to stay. They have a choice—to stay or to return. Let's listen in as the narrator relates this encounter between a ghost and his redeemer.

> I saw coming towards us a Ghost who carried something on his shoulder. Like all the ghosts, he was unsubstantial, but they differed from one another as smokes differ. Some had been whitish; this one was dark and oily. What sat on his shoulder was a little red lizard, and it was twitching its tail like a whip and whispering things in his ear. As we caught sight of him he turned his head to the reptile with a snarl of impatience. "Shut up, I tell you!" he said. It wagged its tail

and continued to whisper to him. He ceased snarling, and presently began to smile. Then he turned and started to limp westward, away from the mountains.

"Off so soon?" said a voice.

"Yes, I'm off," said the Ghost. "Thanks for all your hospitality. But it's no good, you see. I told this little chap," (here he indicated the lizard), "that he'd have to be quiet if he came—which he insisted on doing. Of course his stuff won't do here: I realize that. But he won't stop. I shall just have to go home."

"Would you like me to make him quiet?" said the flaming Spirit—an angel, as I now understood.

"Of course I would," said the Ghost.

"Then I will kill him," said the Angel, taking a step forward.

"Oh—ah—look out! You're burning me. Keep away," said the Ghost, retreating.

"Don't you *want* him killed?"

"You didn't say anything about *killing* him at first. I hardly meant to bother you with anything so drastic as that."

"It's the only way," said the Angel, whose burning hands were now very close to the lizard. "Shall I kill it?"

"Well, that's a further question. I'm quite open to consider it, but it's a new point, isn't it? I mean, for the moment I was only thinking about silencing it because up here—well, it's so damned embarrassing."

"May I kill it?"

"Well, there's time to discuss that later."

"There is no time. May I kill it?"

"Honestly, I don't think there's the slightest necessity for that. I'm sure I shall be able to keep it in order now. I think the gradual process would be far better than killing it."

"The gradual process is of no use at all."

"Don't you think so? Well, I'll think over what you've said very carefully. I honestly will. In fact I'd let you kill it now, but as a matter of fact I'm not feeling frightfully well today. It would be silly to do it *now*. I'd need to be in good health for the operation. Some other day, perhaps."

"There is no other day. All days are present now."

"Get back! You're burning me. How can I tell you to kill it? You'd kill *me* if you did."

"It is not so."

"Why, you're hurting me now."

"I never said it wouldn't hurt you. I said it wouldn't kill you."[94]

And so the Ghost struggles and equivocates, wishing to be free of the red lizard—a symbol for his lust and for everything we cling to despite the fact that these things prevent us from living fully and freely. He fears the process of change—"you'll kill me!" And he fears

[94] C.S. Lewis, *The Great Divorce* (New York: Simon & Schuster, 1996), p. 96-98.

the change itself—as the Lizard whispered to the Ghost, "You'll be without me forever and ever. It's not natural. How could you live? You'd be only a sort of ghost, not a real man as you are now . . ."[95]

We'll return to see the outcome of the Ghost's dilemma in chapter ten. For now, we see that, like Pharaoh, like the Israelites, like us, the Ghost dives and dodges in his efforts to resist change. Like Pharaoh and the Israelites and like us, he must choose change. No one can force that choice, and no one can make it easy. I often find myself discussing this fact with my clients. The Shadow within or the plagues without can disturb our equilibrium and upset the system's homeostasis, but they only create an opportunity for change. Therapy can show us the choice and encourage us to make it in the direction of healing and wholeness—but it can't force the choice or even eliminate all fear of it. To change we must choose, something we'll explore in the next chapter on the Red Sea.

Here, it is only important to say that our fears of the process of change as well as of the unknown territory we will enter are huge—and in ways valid! "It will kill me!" We fear we will no longer be "a real man" or a kind woman or a dutiful child or a person of faith. We ask who we will become if we choose change. Perhaps we will become something rich, but certainly we will become something, to our old selves, strange.

We also fear the reaction of others. Years before the therapy session in which Sylvie wrestled with the brown lump, she was hospitalized for depression and suicidal thoughts. Yet when she left the hospital and came back to therapy, her first question was, "Will anyone think I'm beautiful if I change?" She was voicing the fear we all share: that we'll be alone, rejected, abandoned—or perhaps worse—if we change.

---

[95] Ibid. p. 99.

In fact, others will react, as we will see. Choosing to change patterns of relationships with loved ones is inextricably caught up with the intrapsychic change we've been exploring, one sort of change instigating the other, backward and forward, upward and downward, inside and out.

Changing in Relationships

A lot is at stake when it comes to changing within our relationships. We may use different words to describe our concerns when the relationships are professional rather than personal, but the same issues are at stake. As Sylvie articulated so well, "Will anyone want me if I change?" Will I hurt loved ones or offend colleagues? Will I lose them? Am I becoming selfish, or mean, or weak? If I leave this lonely or abusive relationship, will I be able to survive in the world? Will I find another job or lover? Will I ever want to? Instead of risking this, we ignore problems until they erupt. Then, like the Ghost with his Lizard, in shame and anxiety, we go back to pushing the problems and the pain out of our awareness again. Often we begin to look at our lives and our relationships only when forced to by some external event, our own personal version of an Exodus plague. Some say, for example, that couples often seek therapy for marital problems five years too late.

The Newly Engaged

"My happiness isn't his responsibility—but he'll feel bad if I feel bad, and then I feel bad!" This attractive young couple had not sought marital therapy five years too late. They were newly engaged, in their early twenties, but they were stuck. "I guess we're here because I have a lot of problems sleeping and a lot of nightmares. A couple of years ago, I was sexually assaulted." Josh spoke up, "I wanted to find a way to help Cindy. I tried everything, being there for her constantly—I ran out of things I could do! I'd get frustrated, and maybe it would show and hurt her. I just don't know what to do."

"My mom is frustrated with me, too," Cindy's eyes were tearful as she spoke. "She says, 'You think too much! Keep busy and keep moving on.' Then I feel really guilty and ashamed because I'm not functioning the way Mom would—I feel weak."

As they talked, I realized that, hurtful as it was in and of itself, the sexual assault had exacerbated problems that had already been playing out in their lives. Cindy had not yet finished college despite her obvious brilliance and many gifts. Her attempt to leave home to go to school—before the assault—had ended when she succumbed to family pressure. Living at home since then, she spent a lot of her time hanging out at Josh's apartment or running errands for her mother or grandmother. Josh was successful though bored in a job he didn't like, but it provided financial security for himself and, he hoped, eventually for Cindy. They were leaders in their small start-up church that catered to second and third generation Asian American young people, but Josh had begun to question a God who not only allowed the assault, but also didn't respond to his fervent prayers that Cindy be healed of her emotional pain, insomnia, and nightmares.

Their relationship was one that family systems theorists would call "enmeshed." Each felt the other's feelings and each felt responsible for the other's feelings—a state that appears loving but in fact undermines a healthy self for each of them. Cindy became fearful, depressed, and withdrawn when she felt Josh was disapproving of her in his efforts to help her, or when she felt guilty that her own feelings and perceptions were distressing to him. Josh became critical and upset when he felt left alone and unimportant as she lost herself in helping others or withdrew into depression. Their fears were being triggered by the other's defensive patterns—a painful but self-sustaining feedback loop.

It was clear that the sexual assault, a cruel fraternity prank in a college parking lot, was gaining power from interlocking systems that needed changing. Those interlocking systems were operating on two levels: the intrapsychic systems within both Cindy and Josh, and the interpersonal systems of their relationship to each other, to their families—particularly Cindy's—and to their community of faith. To better understand those systems, let's begin by considering their histories, the childhood problems and solutions that became their Egypts.

Childhood Problems and Childhood Solutions

As this bright and loving couple began sharing about their lives, it became clear that both had experienced difficult and surprisingly similar childhoods. Both grew up with immigrant parents who were struggling to make a life in a new country. Josh's father was rigidly obsessive and physically abusive—Cindy's mother was extremely controlling and punitive.

Cindy's parents insisted that their daughter honor their wishes in ways that went beyond the filial piety valued by their culture. An eight-year-old Cindy would be left standing alone in the corner of the kitchen after the family had gone to bed for the night because she had not eaten her dinner. Her mother had cooked that dinner after she returned from work, often serving it at 10:00 or 11:00 pm. Though she was an A-student in school, caring with friends, and active in her church, her parents did not seem to value her academic goals and achievements as they did her brother's. Pressed into working in her family's business, shamed when her needs conflicted with her mother's, expected to serve as hostess with family and friends, Cindy had come to believe that her only worth was to serve and that to love was to give herself away. Her Christian faith seemed to reinforce the truth of this belief. When no one needed her, she would try to do her homework by burning the midnight oil until she was exhausted in the wee hours of the morning. Then she would collapse in hopeless depression, withdrawing from everyone and everything until she felt well enough to begin the cycle again. Cindy was a Cinderella in her own home.

Not surprisingly, Cindy had suffered for years with painful gastrointestinal problems. The family system affects the psychological system affects the physiological system. A bit like Pharaoh, though unintentionally so, her parents tried to maintain the family system and cope with Cindy. She was sent away to live with relatives in China during high school—her parents said that her stress and rebellion would decrease away from school, sports, church, and family. "They said I couldn't come home until I was better." Feeling blamed and in exile, lectured at by well-meaning relatives, Cindy learned even more strictly to be compliant and to hide her true feelings and needs. That earned her a ticket home but sunk her deeper into the family system. Cut off from expressing or acknowledging her feelings and desires even to herself, she began to lose her motivation and sense of direction in life. She began to internalize her family's view that she was weak and couldn't manage on her own.

Josh described his father's discipline as "very weird—if we didn't make our beds, he'd throw the blankets downstairs and then the mattress. He'd pop our balloons, confiscate toys, hit us, and yell 'you're not smart!'" His father would demand moment-by-moment accountings of time spent and planned. He had nearly bitten off the tiny finger of his older sister when she was an infant—threw her against the wall when she was older. His parents' fighting and unhappiness eventually resulted in their divorce when Josh was in high school—a time when Josh had found meaning in the encouragement of his teachers and the faith of his church.

As a kid in the midst of the family violence, Josh found refuge in sleep. He often found himself alone in the chaos of the household, feeling unimportant to anyone, learning to take care of himself. The messages he absorbed were that life is chaotic and uncertain so you must take care of yourself—that love means protecting the other from pain in hopes of preserving their ability to love you—that anger and male power are dangerous and selfish. In response to these lessons, Josh learned to withdraw from risks and to close down in the face of anger—whether his own or someone else's. He learned to be careful and controlled, caring and controlling, and very independent. He wanted to be Prince Charming to Cindy's Cinderella, rescuing her from the evils in her family and in the world, especially the world of sexually predatory men.

Systems, Feedback Loops and Adult Problems

This context gave Cindy's traumatic assault its power and meaning. Old lessons were being reinforced, old fears exacerbated. Cindy learned again that she was weak, and that any effort to achieve her own goals would be attacked, that her life and even her body were for the use of others. Josh learned again that male power is dangerous and selfish; that you must take care of yourself, and that you must protect your loved ones so that you can be loved.

Operating on these beliefs and in his wish to claim and protect the woman he loved from the intrusive or abusive interest of other men, Josh inadvertently had contributed to Cindy's feelings of insecurity and inadequacy. His own anxiety drove him to criticize her when he thought her clothing was too sexy or her willingness to help her male friends too generous. Even his wish to be there for her, to help her and to put his own life aside if she needed it, subtly communicated that he doubted her ability to help herself.

The system was self-reinforcing. In response to Josh, Cindy felt helpless and weak in a dangerous world in which she could not trust her own judgment or perceptions. Again, she felt that her only purpose was to serve his needs. Again, her motivation and sense of direction for her life were undermined. She was complying with his control and pushing down her own power, ambition, and anger and re-experiencing these aspects of herself in violent nightmares. Like Moses before his encounter with the burning bush, Cindy had long ago learned to fear and deny her passion and her power, her Shadow side. Meanwhile, repressing her drive for individual expression was giving tremendous power to her Shadow—it was raging in the nightmares that in turn stymied all of Josh's efforts to help her and to enable them to build a life together.

The interpersonal and intrapsychic systems in which they lived, their Egypts, were dominated by the values of compliance and security as a way to live, of control and caretaking as a way to love. Early efforts to step outside this system had met with harsh punishment. As a result, each was struggling to accomplish their individual developmental tasks of launching into life, into a career that fit, and into respectful and reciprocal relationships. The demand for compliance meant they struggled to know themselves, since it required that they discredit and ignore their own perceptions, thoughts, and desires. The insistence on security meant they were afraid to risk expressing themselves in the world in case they gambled and lost. Love as caretaking was, in fact, disrespectful of the strength and individuality of the other, further eroding their confidence. They were coming to recognize the risks they needed to take to change things. As Josh put it, "It's like we're learning similar lessons: you have to allow others to suffer sometimes," trusting that the other *can* find their own way, believing in them when you may least believe in them.

The sexual assault not only gained power from its relational context, but ultimately it was the plague that drove them into counseling, into facing the changes that needed to be made in the systems in which they were each stuck. This young couple had the wisdom and faith to allow the assault to open them to deeper change and healing, both for themselves as individuals and for their future marriage, their families, and their church.

Sandals and Unleavened Bread

In therapy, Cindy and Josh and I were like the Israelites on the night of the Passover. We began to prepare for a departure from Egypt. We listened to their life stories, bearing witness to the trauma of the sexual assault and to the childhood traumas that preceded it. We began to untangle and understand their childhood problems and solutions and the way these contributed to the frustrations and problems in their relationship to each other. Things began to change. The sexual assault quickly lost its power as Cindy took back hers. She began to take her power back from Josh's "protection," recognizing the need and fear in Josh that gave it such controlling intensity. She took her power back from her mother by trusting her own perspective and judgment. The nightmares ceased. The beautiful China doll mask that she had worn early in therapy, bland and blind-eyed, gave way to sparkling eyes and an animated expression. In session, she enjoyed sharing her keen insight and clear perspective on herself, others, and her relationships. She began to get excited about the future, dreaming about graduate school and a career.

Josh began thinking about his own career. He discussed the risk of giving up the security of an engineering salary for a calling to be an inner city middle school teacher. He talked about the teachers who had made such a difference in his life. He described the friend whose Oakland junior high school students struck cool poses for the class photo but still had big smiles on their faces. He read books on God's call, the risk it required, and wrestled with the need for security that held him back.

The couple began to shift in their relationship to their church. They wondered about healthy boundaries within the congregation. They questioned the leadership role they felt pressed into and the mission and theology of their church itself. They noticed discrepancies and sometimes wondered about the motivations of some of their pastors. They wanted to explore a different view of what it means to serve and to believe.

The plague of the sexual assault had brought about a situation in which this couple could not avoid the deeper problems that had held them captive. Now the real work began. Systems hate change. Parents and even pastors began to react. Like Pharaoh, they didn't like the changes. Like Pharaoh, they didn't want to let the couple go. Unlike Pharaoh, they wanted to protect Josh and Cindy from mistakes and hurt. They expressed their concerns. They lectured. They asked for prayer. Cindy's folks said, "Don't expect much—the world isn't good." Everyone said they were worried about Cindy.

Cindy began to be afraid of the changes she recognized in herself and felt guilty at the pain these changes were inflicting or perhaps would inflict on loved ones. Anxiety and guilt trigger a powerful pull toward homeostasis. Cindy's nightmares returned. She said, "I feel like a scrambled egg when I leave them: pastors, Josh, my family! I acclimate to whomever I'm talking to! I'm so good at doing what people want. I'm angry and I avoid them—or I decide I'm gonna stir them up, but then I become compliant. I think that there's nothing inside me, no self—or worse, there's someone others don't like, someone mean and inconsiderate." During our therapy hours, I worried that *I* might become one whose influence turned her into a scrambled egg! I hunkered down in my chair, guarding my input as I watched for the mask or the sparkle that would show us when her true, alive self appeared. Seeing Cindy's turmoil and depression return, Josh said, "Cindy has no job and no schooling! We're making no progress!" Cindy said, "I don't know who to trust!"

Josh and Cindy were like the Israelites, excited by the promise of freedom and a new life, and then terrified by the reaction of Pharaoh. They were like the Israelites eating their Passover meal, reeling from plagues and unsure of where to go. The sexual assault, Cindy's nightmares, and Josh's inability to help her were all events pushing them forward toward change. Yet as they began to change their ways of being in the world, they were assaulted in new ways: by their own guilt and fear, and by the concerned and combined onslaught of their loved ones. Systems hate change and will not let us go easily.

The Tragic and Transformation

In the Exodus story, an escalating series of external events, beginning with the inconvenient and ending with the tragic, forced a system into disequilibrium. It was as though Egypt and Israel both need to be pried loose from the status quo, the first stage on the transformative journey. A sexual assault forced disequilibrium in the intrapsychic and interpersonal systems in which Cindy and Josh lived. So many times, it is an external event that pushes us to grow and to change. We are forced out of the nest, pushed onto the road. The door is slammed shut behind us. Sometimes these events are desired and sought: a wedding, a baby, retirement, but many times these external events are unwelcome. Sometimes they are tragic. Often, they are not our intention—nor our fault.

In saying that the tragic can push us onto the road toward transformation, a difficult and troubling issue must be addressed. We are in an inescapable bind the moment we say that tragic circumstances can lead to transformation and wholeness. Does it mean that we are somehow rationalizing the suffering of the innocent? Because these horrible events happen, does it mean that God is either a sadist or non-existent? Theologians and atheists wrestle with these questions, but clinical experience and personal witness join to affirm that suffering "the slings and arrows of outrageous fortune"[96] can be transformative.

People are surprisingly clear about this . . . later. Cameron Clapp is a shining example. When he was fifteen years old, he'd been partying with his friends. Falling asleep on some railroad tracks, he was hit by a train. He lost both legs and one of his arms. Now at twenty-three, he balanced on prosthetic limbs as he walked along those same railroad tracks with Bill Whitaker, his interviewer.[97] Finishing college, he also traveled around the country talking to veterans and other amputees and taking part in swimming, running, and golf competitions. Whitaker finally said, "I've got to ask. If you could have your arm and legs back today, would you?" Cameron said, "Honestly, I would not want my legs and arm back. I wouldn't be the person I am today."

Sheldon Vanauken wrote an autobiographical story of his love for his wife, Davy, and her tragic death. They had pledged themselves to cultivate an extraordinary love. For many years this was their highest goal. Then, during a period of study at Oxford, they found themselves attracted to and finally giving themselves up to a greater love, the love of God. They met and developed a friendship with C.S. Lewis. When Davy died of a mysterious disease, Vanauken confronted the horrible "why?" of her death. Although the events of the book took place in the decades during and after World War II, it was not until 1977 that Vanauken wrote his book, *A Severe Mercy*. "It was death—Davy's death—that was the severe mercy . . . . That death, so full of suffering for us both, suffering that still overwhelmed my life, was yet a severe mercy. A mercy as severe as death, a severity

---

[96] Shakespeare, *Hamlet*, 3.1.65
[97] CBS, "The Bionic Man," April 25, 2006. See also Cameron's website: cameronclapp.com.

as merciful as love." [98] He had begun to consider her death, horrible and painful as it was, as a grace that prevented greater horror and pain should his jealous determination to have an extraordinary love destroy all other good. He wrote, "Nothing now could mar our love: the manuscript has now gone to the printer."[99] He had come to see the tragic death of his wife as an external event, like the plagues in the Exodus story, that forced him toward growth and change in needed ways—for himself and for her.

The priest and poet Gerard Manley Hopkins, who died in 1889 at the young age of forty-five, suffered from depression, isolation, and probably from a deep and lonely conflict over his sexuality. In the midst of our suffering—whether from a plague without or the Shadow within—he gives voice to our cry of pain and protest.

His poetry is revolutionary in its use of grammar and diction and his coining of new words—but if you read it by letting it flow over your mind like clear water over the pebbled bed of a stream, its sense is moving and powerful. In his poem, *Carrion Comfort*, he struggles not to give into depression and hopelessness and a desire for suicide. He uses the metaphor of a wrestling match with an opponent first pictured as a dangerous beast, then as a hero "whose heaven-handling flung me"—and expresses for us what it is to be in the midst of those experiences we fear might destroy us, our plagues. His poem communicates the great pain and almost hysterical panic we feel in the midst of such suffering.

---

[98] Sheldon Vanauken, *A Severe Mercy* (San Francisco: HarperCollins Publishers, 1977), p. 211. The title of the book is from a comment of C.S. Lewis to Vanauken. Written as encouragement, it was taken from an expression in one of Charles Williams' novels.
[99] Ibid. p. 183.

Something Rich and Strange:

Carrion Comfort

Not, I'll not, carrion comfort, Despair, not feast on thee;

Not untwist—slack they may be—these last strands of man

In me or, most weary, cry *I can no more.* I can;

Can something, hope, wish day come, not choose not to be.

But ah, but O thou terrible, why wouldst thou rude on me

Thy wring-world right foot rock? Lay a lionlimb against
  me? Scan

With darksome devouring eyes my bruised bones? And fan,

O in turns of tempest, me heaped there; me frantic to
  avoid thee and flee?

Why? That my chaff might fly; my grain lie, sheer and clear.

Nay in all that toil, that coil, since (seems) I kissed the rod,

Hand rather, my heart lo! Lapped strength, stole joy, would
  laugh, cheer.

Cheer whom though? The hero whose heaven-handling
  flung me, foot trod

Me? Or me that fought him? O which one? Is it each one?

  That night, that year

Of now done darkness I wretch lay wrestling with (my
  God!) my God.[100]

[100] Gerard Manley Hopkins, *The Poems of Gerard Manley Hopkins*, ed. W.H. Gardner & N.H. MacKenzie (Oxford: Oxford University Press, 4th edition, 1967), p. 99-100.

Hopkins cries, as we do, "Why?" The answer he gives is that this is what separates the chaff of his character from the grain—a metaphor of transformation—but in the poem, one that sounds academic and flat even if true. Any answer to the question "why?" falls flat and fails to comfort when we are in the midst of such turmoil and pain. More emotionally resonant is the assertion that in the midst of his suffering, he finds strength, joy, even laughter as he battles, *because* he battles. He cheers the wrestlers on. He suggests that even in the midst of the agonizing and lonely process there are times of exhilaration and joy—and that when it is over and he looks back, he finds with amazement that it was "(my God!) my God" with whom he wrestled.

This imagery reminds me of the story of Jacob wrestling with the angel until the break of day—an allusion surely intended by this priestly scholar. "Your name is no longer Jacob. From now on it's Israel (God-Wrestler); you've wrestled with God and you've come through."[101] In the wrestling match with God, through the process of transformation and especially in those moments of suffering and pain brought on by external events, plagues, that force us out of our comfort zones, what happens? For Cameron Clapp with his prosthetic limbs, Hopkins the poet-priest, Vanauken the widower, and Jacob, now called Israel, what happened was a transformation so fundamental that it was about being and selfhood and identity—the ancient Hebrew metaphor is that of a changed name. "I wouldn't be the person I am today."

Painful as it is to reel and recoil from these plagues in our own lives, it is also difficult to watch another struggle with them. As therapist or pastor, friend or spouse, parent or child, how can we believe and hope without trying to cut short another's suffering for their sake as well as our own? If we offer suggestions or advice, theologizing or

---

[101] Genesis 32:22-32

help, might we be making everything worse and cutting ourselves off from each other in the process? With Josh, must we learn that "you have to allow others to suffer sometimes"? Answers are of little help. Presence and empathy are needed, and to offer these requires our own faith and our own experience of the transformative process.

From inside people's life stories, we discover that the tragic can become the transformative, and that the transformation can be considered worth the pain. We can become someone we respect and enjoy. We can learn what we didn't know. We can experience what we would not have expected or sought. We can love those we never knew, and we can discover the God whose name is "I-Am-Present." To believe this doesn't take away the fear, the pain, and the suffering—but it can bring hope and meaning to them. To believe this doesn't mean we should try to convince others or even ourselves of the truth of it in moments of tragedy—but it can give us the capacity to bear witness to the process.

Josh and Cindy show us how to engage that process, to allow an external event, a plague, to open ourselves to deeper healing. Yet the journey has just begun. In leaving their old systems and challenging their old learnings, both within themselves and in their families and their community of faith, they have reached a perilous point in their journey. Like the Israelites, Cindy and Josh are camped at the Red Sea.

The distresses of choice are our chance to be blessed.
W.H. Auden

"Tell the people to go forward!"
God

Chapter Six:
The Red Sea

Mount Olympus stands midway between Athens and Thessaloniki and between the Aegean and the Adriatic Seas. At 9,576 feet high, it is said that you can see the curvature of the earth from the top, and I can attest that it is true. I was just twenty-two years old and hiking up Olympus through evergreen forests and meadows of wild flowers. We stayed in a shelter near the top for the night, between rough wool blankets with no sheets to soften them, then tackled the peak on our hands and knees the next morning. I was glad to hover close to the loose rocks that cascaded down the mountain at our footsteps, and very glad when we left our names in the book at the top and began the descent. Soon we reached the footpath again and began to walk down the mountain.

A steep rock wall rose at my right hand while the slope to my left descended steeply to the sea. I could see Turkey hazy beyond that sea. Then the rock wall on my right fell away, and I could see another sea and beyond it—Italy. With Italy on my right and Turkey on my left, the curvature of the earth between—suddenly a crevasse appeared in the path ahead. Only fifteen feet deep and perhaps two feet wide, I could cross it easily with a single step, but at that dizzying height, on that exposed rock spine, I felt panic rising. One step and I would be across—but for the moment I could not take that step. I thought about turning around and going back the way we'd come the previous day. I thought about my hiking companion already some distance ahead of me. I knew that if I didn't take that step *right now*, I never would.

And so I stepped. As Robert Frost says, "that has made all the difference."[102] On that mountaintop, I experienced a moment of choice—one requiring a decision of the will—like that which confronts anyone on a journey of transformative change. In the story of the Exodus, the children of Israel confronted the same moment of choice at the Red Sea. It had seemed as though they were home free, or at least free at last, when they left their homes in Goshen, but now, with Egypt behind and the wilderness of the Sinai ahead, panic struck. A choice had to be made.

The Exodus Story

The Israelites left Egypt—lock, stock, and barrel—with their children, their livestock, and their neighbor's jewelry. Any map will show that there was a more direct route to the Promised Land of Canaan than they the one they actually took. The Scriptures say, "God didn't lead them by the road through the land of the Philistines, which was the shortest route, for God thought, 'If the people encounter war, they'll change their minds and go back to Egypt.' So God led the people on the wilderness road, looping around to the Red Sea."[103]

---

[102] Robert Frost, *The Road Not Taken, Robert Frost's Poems* (New York: St. Martin's Press, 1971), p. 219.
[103] Exodus 13:17-18

Can we imagine the scene? 600,000 people with their animals and their possessions kicked up the dust of the desert as they moved slowly away from their homes. 600,000 people who had been slaves—used to obeying, used to being cared for—faced the unknown of the wilderness and of a future on their own. Yet they were not alone. "The Pillar of Cloud by day and the Pillar of Fire by night never left the people"[104] as God continued to make good on a new name, I-Am-Present. Step by unknown step, the Israelites were led in the specific details of their daily lives.

Meanwhile, the system still hated change. Pharaoh had second thoughts. He hitched up his chariots and went after the Israelites. Indeed, the thought of reorganizing Egypt without their masses of slave labor must have been daunting. An example from our own more recent history comes to mind: reconstruction of the American south after the Civil War. Almost one hundred fifty years later, we are still experiencing the results of the choices made then. Ancient Egypt must have trembled in the face of a similar challenge.

In Exodus 14 we read a story so fascinating to Hollywood and so impossible for modern scriptwriters to improve.

> The Egyptians gave chase and caught up with them where they had made camp by the sea—all Pharaoh's horse-drawn chariots and their riders, all his foot soldiers there at Pi Hahiroth opposite Baal Zephon.
>
> As Pharaoh approached, the Israelites looked up and saw them—Egyptians! Coming at them!
>
> They were totally afraid. They cried out in terror to God. They told Moses, "Weren't the cemeteries large enough in Egypt so that you had to take us out here in the wilderness

---

[104] Exodus 13:22

to die? What have you done to us, taking us out of Egypt? Back in Egypt didn't we tell you this would happen? Didn't we tell you, 'Leave us alone here in Egypt—we're better off as slaves in Egypt than as corpses in the wilderness.'"[105]

600,000 people panicked and, in their panic, blaming. Can we blame them? Behind them the dust cloud raised by the Egyptian army—before them the shallow but expansive waters of the Red, or Reed, Sea and beyond that the rocky, barren wilderness of the Sinai. They were cornered. Moses found it hard to contain their terror and perhaps his own, to soothe and calm, to continue to guide. Indeed, he had no answer but faith: "'Don't be afraid. Stand firm and watch God do his work of salvation for you today . . . God will fight the battle for you.'"[106]

Back at his tent, Moses himself must have been afraid and crying out to God! God, what are you doing? And more urgently, what shall we do? It was a moment—much larger, but still something like the one I experienced on Mount Olympus—a moment of terrible exposure, terrifying to go forward, but to go back . . . .

God answered, perhaps with some exasperation.

"Moses, why do you cry to me? Tell the people to go forward!"[107]

Why do you cry to me? Tell the people to go forward. Only one step across the crevasse, go forward. In the midst of terror and confusion, go forward. Into the unknown and unpredictable, go forward. No longer knowing why you are doing it, go forward!

---

[105] Exodus 14:8-12
[106] Exodus 14:13-14
[107] Exodus 14:15, NRSV

The Pillar of Cloud and Fire now moved between the Israelites and the Egyptians as they camped near each other by the sea that night. An east wind came up and blew all night long, a miraculous wind that drove the shallow waters of the sea back. The Israelites went forward on foot straight across the mucky seabed. The Egyptians chased them, but rich in their chariots and their horses, the hooves and narrow wheel rims could not navigate the swampy mud. It was now their turn to panic, stuck in the muck and the mud. As the morning sun rose and the land began to heat up, the wind ceased. "The waters returned, drowning the chariots and riders of Pharaoh's army that had chased after Israel into the sea. Not one of them survived."[108]

On the other side, watching the terrible army caught and covered by the waters of the sea, the Israelites were beside themselves with amazement. Thrilled! Glad! Praising God and Moses. Miriam, Moses and Aaron's sister, sang and danced with her tambourine, and all the women joined her. Wonderful! As Martin Luther King Jr. cried out in a similar moment, the children of Israel were now indeed "free at last, free at last, thank God Almighty, we are free at last!"[109]

The drama of the story carries us with its heroic moment of choice, its narrow escape, and its miracle, but at the heart of the story is a very simple instruction: "Tell the people to go forward." How does that very simple and very difficult instruction fit into what psychologists have learned and taught about the process of change?

---

[108] Exodus 14:28
[109] Martin Luther King, quoting an old spiritual in his "I Have A Dream" speech, given at the Lincoln Memorial on August 28, 1963.

Risking Psychological Healing

Irvin Yalom, brilliant and respected Stanford psychiatry professor and existential psychotherapist, has written a wonderful book entitled, *The Art of Therapy*. In it he writes that "effective psychotherapy consists of an alternating sequence: evocation and experiencing of affect followed by analysis and integration of affect."[110] He is referring to the affect or emotion we bring to therapy: perhaps the pain of old trauma, the frustration of our current situation, the longing for connection and self-expression. For therapy to be effective, it must involve *both* experiencing and then understanding.

In therapy we come to understand many things in general: how symptoms and problems come about, how the brain, body, and the mind work, how change happens. We learn specific tools and techniques that can be implemented to help and to heal. We also come to understand many things in particular: how we each have arrived at the place we find ourselves in life, our Egypts, what is going on in *our* brains and *our* minds, how we learned to cope and what results from some of our particular defensive patterns, what choices we have that we did not realize we had.

In the end, understanding is not enough. No therapy that consists of ideas and insight alone is enough to create change. We must also *experience* something—within the therapy hour and outside in the real world, and in order to experience anything, we must choose to risk, to face what we most fear. We must go forward—or go back only to face the same or perhaps a more difficult choice again. How can we do this when our feelings are rising up in protest?

The ancient Greeks conceived of human psychology in terms of three primary faculties: Reason, Will, and Passion. I'm reminded

---

[110] Irvin D. Yalom, *The Gift of Therapy* (New York: HarperCollins Publishers, 2002), p. 71.

of the three principle characters of the early Star Trek series: Mr. Spock, Captain Kirk, and Dr. McCoy.[111] May the Trekkies among us consider who they would prefer to have in the captain's chair on the Starship Enterprise during a Klingon attack. Dr. McCoy brought emotion, compassion, and passion. He would be all feeling, his mind full of images of pain and death and horror. Mr. Spock was Vulcan, a race that had disciplined itself to pure reason—except for one Bacchanalian revel every seven years. He would be logical, his mind full of facts and figures and historical precedents. I might prefer Spock to command the ship, but only if Captain James T. Kirk were not at hand. Spock and Bones fought constantly, but Kirk could listen to McCoy's passionate concern and Spock's logical reasoning—and then decide. Kirk personifies what the ancient Greeks called will, the capacity to intend and to choose. Given our understanding of the facts and given our understanding of our feelings, we can choose—then and only then do our feelings calm down and come around, something like Dr. McCoy might do after the Klingon attack is repulsed and the crisis is over. The next time he might be calmer and more confident, even during the battle—the time after perhaps even before the battle!

Recently I was sharing some of these ideas with one of my patients. He said, "Yes . . . if you're afraid—say in combat or something—you may never *feel* brave, but you can still do courageous acts." We can choose, despite our feelings, to act in ways that we believe are right. Our feelings inform our choices but do not necessarily change until after our choices have been made, until *after* we have experienced something new. To experience anything new, we must choose to go forward into the unknown, as a decision of the will.

Psychologists have found that this is true in extensive research in the laboratory and in the consulting room as they have sought specific

---

[111] "Star Trek," written and produced by Gene Roddenberry, premiered on NBC in 1966, ran for only three seasons, but became a cult classic.

therapy approaches for specific problems. Let's consider a single recalcitrant but "simple" psychiatric diagnosis to understand how this works—simple phobias.

Simple Phobias

As anyone who has one can tell you, simple phobias are not all that simple. By "simple," psychologists mean that these phobias are fears of very specific objects, animals, or situations—they exclude fears of people and social situations, or fears that result from trauma. Heights or water, spiders, snakes, or sharks, being confined in a tight space or flying in an airplane all constitute common phobic objects—but anything can become a phobic stimulus. Often the phobic stimuli are objects or situations that are inherently dangerous to humans, but a phobic fear goes beyond what we know is reasonably warranted. It can become crippling. Often we have no idea why we fear a particular thing, though sometimes we remember when we learned to fear it.

In the 1950s, psychologist Joseph Wolpe developed a treatment for phobic anxiety that he called systematic desensitization. Building on the classical conditioning discoveries of Pavlov and others, he theorized that by pairing a specific behavioral action, relaxation, with the specific phobic stimulus—let's say flying in an airplane—he could reduce or even eliminate (the technical term is "extinguish") the anxious reaction. His technique involves learning how to relax one's body, constructing "an anxiety hierarchy" from least to most anxiety-provoking situation, and then stepping gradually up the hierarchy, relaxing at each stage before moving to the next. This can begin in imagination and then move to "in vivo" real life situations. At its heart, this technique is about choosing to confront what you fear, about "going forward."

Let me tell you the story of my daughter Kristen and her fear of flying. A shaky and tearful ten-year-old came home from a trip to visit her grandparents one summer. She had vomited from Athens across the Atlantic, transferred by wheelchair to a new airplane in New York, and then threw up across the United States to San Francisco. Everyone concluded that she was afraid of flying or had motion sickness, and I concluded that it was all because I hadn't been there. After all, her favorite childhood activity was twirling round and round on the monkey bars. Cars and boats never gave her a moment's pause. How could this be motion sickness?

Over the next few years she took a few more flights—as it happened, never with me—and threw up throughout the entire flight from start to finish, soup to nuts, every time. When my predoctoral internship arrived, moving to Honolulu for a year meant a five-hour flight across the Pacific—and back. I took control of the situation, holding her hand and reassuring her that all would be well, smug in my superiority as her most secure attachment object, counting on the mommy factor. We drove to the airport, checked in, and walked to the gate. I noticed she looked a little grey. Her hand was getting cold as ice. We boarded the plane, but before we even sat down, she tossed her cookies into, unfortunately, her neighbor's seat! A little dashed and more than puzzled, I discovered that the smell of the airplane diesel, the smell of the food on board, and her awareness of the length of the trip were all triggering her nausea. Upon further investigation, it turned out that before the first airsick trip, she'd had chicken for lunch in the Athens airport. Food poisoning, not motion sickness, had triggered her initial eighteen-hour vomiting. Unfortunately, the sensations associated with flying had become intensely associated with that nausea and now triggered it all on their own. She had become afraid of flying.

During the next year, we had a number of opportunities to work through her anxiety hierarchy. We practiced relaxation techniques and created an audiotape: walking in imagination through the process of leaving for the airport, driving along the Kalanianaole Highway, hearing the roar of the planes taking off, smelling the diesel, boarding, flying, and landing. Then we had the opportunity to practice in the real world—a trip to Maui. From the small commuter terminal with no long hallways to walk, Kristen had only a forty-five minute trip with no food served and with Mom in the seat next to her. (I was still working that mommy factor!) We went, we boarded, we flew, we landed, and we did not vomit! She was a little green around the gills, but triumphant when we emerged into the fragrant tropical breeze and the hot sunshine of the Valley Isle.

We had a couple of other trips that year to Kauai and to the Big Island. No food, short flights—each time she got a little more confident and a little less nauseated. Then came the next step: the trip home to California, five hours, and food served on board. We packed her a lunch so she didn't have to eat their food, rented a headset for the movie, and this time no mommy factor, as I stayed another month to complete my internship. Again, triumph! As I write this, my daughter is twenty-six years old, a veteran traveler of the world: Greece, of course, and Chile, Ecuador, Montana, Hawaii—all by herself. She will even eat the airplane food . . . if they have a vegetarian entrée! Systematic desensitization worked as she thought through the realities of the problem and then chose—a decision of her will—to confront her fear, step by more anxious step, and in that experience discovered she could conquer it. Then and only then did her feelings, both emotional and physical, fall in line with her will and her reason. She went forward.

Fears that must be confronted to be healed—these underlay Kristen's fear of flying as they do many other problems, including depression, panic, long-term interpersonal problems, substance abuse, sleep disorders, and even some health problems and chronic pain. As we approach what we fear—having thought it through, despite our feelings, and choose to move forward by an act of will—those difficult and painful feelings begin to subside. Choosing to confront these fears and anxieties constitutes the Red Sea that must be crossed to continue our journey of transformation. It always requires courage and stubborn persistence, a longing for health and wholeness and love that is strong enough to overcome the fear of what is known and what is unknown. "Tell the people to go forward!"

Bernadette did not struggle with a fear of flying. She was reluctantly in the midst of a divorce, yet the choice that faced her, her Red Sea, was exactly the same as Kristen's. To go forward, she had to choose to confront what she most feared.

The Reluctant Divorcée

"I'd like to give you the whole story. There was a time I was frustrated with William. He hasn't been happy." She went on to describe her husband's long sequence of affairs, "his compartmentalizing" his life to accommodate his love for her while continuing relationships with other women—"and he doesn't know why." "My husband and I are on the verge of divorce—I think I need to move forward, but emotionally I'm so connected to him!"

So began Bernadette's therapy, separated from her husband and already camped in front of the Red Sea. She had been shaken from her safe and secure Egypt: staying home with her children, being well provided for by a man she loved and who took care of her, enjoying her friends and family, volunteering in her parish church and school. The plague that drove her out was her husband's repeated infidelity despite couples therapy for them and individual therapy for him.

As with Cindy and Josh, this plague forced her to confront the ways that her childhood solutions to real problems had become her adult problem. The youngest of five children, her alcoholic parents frequently fought, often about money, and had separated temporarily during her second grade year. Alcoholism, "womanizing," and depression were themes in the lives of both sets of her grandparents, generational patterns now playing out in her life. She said she felt "weak and defective" to see her childhood exerting an influence on her now.

Yet she slowly and courageously began to work through her painful childhood memories. She was the lonely little girl who put her head under the covers but kept her hand lifted out so that Jesus could take her to heaven if she died. She was the little girl who found her mother passed out drunk on the front porch—"I felt safe with her when she wasn't drinking! I'd hope . . . but then she was drunk again." She was Daddy's little girl whose beloved father was so much fun and so loving, but who fell down drunk by the side of the path on a father-daughter camp out. She was the little girl who adored her big brothers and sister—and who was heartbroken as one by one they escaped that home to find their own lives. Her childhood solution to these problems was to cultivate her faith, but also her fantasies, and to be the kind of sweet and loving little girl others would want to care for without her asking them.

"I fought my whole life to stay on the functional side of life—with William, I thought I'd made it." William gave her the life she had always wanted . . . on the surface. She never had to worry about money, they had three beautiful little boys, and William assured her she would always be able to stay home with them and be cared for by him. He gave her the fantasy, asking only that she not see what else was happening in their lives and not speak up or ask too much of him.

Bernadette's therapeutic task was exactly to choose to see and to speak. The fear she needed to confront was of what would happen if she saw what was real and gave up the fantasy, if she spoke up and asked for what she needed from William, her sons, her friends, even her therapist. She had already begun to confront the reality of her childhood. Now she began to confront the reality of her marriage and her husband's inability or unwillingness to provide more than financial security and a fantasy of their life together. Slowly, she began to confront the reality that she was alone in the world, alone as in her childhood experience and in her greatest fear, alone without a safety net and with only herself and God to depend on. Unfortunately, you never know how God will live up to the name I-Am-Present. "If I trust him, he might put me through another trial!" she cried.

Over the course of three long years, Bernadette reluctantly and painfully began to see and to speak. There were lots of by-ways. When you are the single mother of three little boys there are many ways to avoid seeing or speaking. There is Little League and first communion, homework and play dates, ski trips, cooking and washing up, laundry, chauffeuring, and volunteering. The divorce process lingered on, and as long as it did, she did not have to face the final and irrevocable reality that she was on her own, an adult with no one to take care of her or even to share life with her day by day. "I don't know if I have it in me to go through the divorce! I'm so tired! Sometimes I just wish God would take me. I'm so afraid I won't be able to make ends meet! I miss the security William gave me. I feel a pit in my stomach to think of the divorce!"

One session, she shared a dream about "coming here": *"You and I were meeting, and I had my rolling cooler and clothes, and I unpacked it. When it was time to end, I was trying to pack things back up. You opened the door and the next patient walked in! I thought, 'I've got to get packed or Susan will . . . ' You came in and you were nice about it. I finally got it all packed up. I guess I had a lot to off-load! Maybe*

I'm now getting to things I don't understand . . . this fear of being on my own."

I noticed the dream's insecurity in the therapeutic relationship with concern. Her dream revealed something therapists call a negative transference, something that can undermine therapy if ignored but can reinvigorate therapy if we confront it together, experience and understand it, and work it through. So I asked, "What was last session about that got you stirred up this way?"

"Being vulnerable. We talked about how my sister and also William were both there for me—then suddenly they weren't. With William, I gave him everything and thought, *it's safe.* I told him my secrets, that I was damaged goods because of my parents' alcoholism. I've told you my secrets now, and I'm afraid you'll say, 'Well, Bernadette, if you're not trying, if I'm spinning my wheels with you—don't come back!' I'm always aware of your feelings, and want to make things okay for *you!* And there's been a lull in the therapy. I'm not taking that next step in the divorce you and Father Patrick think I should be."

Bernadette's own self-judging feelings, her own impatience with her progress were being projected onto me as she struggled with her decision to go forward. She was becoming truly aware of the Red Sea she'd been camped beside for so long. In the therapeutic relationship, she was testing to see whether I would still be there for her if she weren't pleasing or convenient for me. She was also facing the reality that a loving adult relationship is not the caretaking one that is appropriate for a child with her parent—caretaking she had not gotten in childhood when she needed it but continued to long for now. In other relationships she had begun to risk a little bit of speaking up and asking for what she needed—practicing first with people like salesmen and workmen and later with more important friends. Now she was speaking up with me.

A few weeks later, she came to therapy with a series of dreams which, taken in sequence, can be seen as her fear, her longing, and her courageous solution to that next step dilemma.

First, her fear: *"I took my boys on a ferry to an island where we spent the day. It was time to go back, but there was no ferry—we were to get into inner tubes! But there was a huge waterfall near and I thought, 'How can I get three kids across without going over the waterfall?' Well, I thought I'd try, but there was also a huge wall of water, and first we had to go up and over this. I thought, 'I can't do it alone! I'll lose one or all my kids! I'll just have to stay.'"* Bernadette was terrified she couldn't manage alone, picturing this in imagery that could not be closer to the scene of the children of Israel facing the waters of the Red Sea!

Second, her longing: *"William was there. I looked at him longingly. We had an unspoken bond; I think we hugged. We took the kids to the movies. I held William's hand and felt safe.* You know books and movies are two escapes I loved and love!" Bernadette hungered to feel safely cared for and to escape the harsh realities of her single life.

Third, her solution: *"The boys and I are in Hawaii with a group, we're at the beach and the boys are playing in the waves. I was talking to a woman, and then beyond her I saw my five-year-old Michael coughing and struggling to get back. I hadn't watched, and he can't swim! I tried to tell her, but the words wouldn't come out and my legs wouldn't move either!*

Then I got to him, I was holding him, and a huge twelve-foot wave came up to us. Michael got a huge breath and the wave came over us, then back toward us and we were underwater. It crashed on us, forced us lower—I didn't know which way was

*up. Michael screamed and I thought, 'Don't open your mouth!'
Then a couple of more waves came before I got us to shore. I was
holding him unconscious on the shore—there was no heartbeat
and no breath. I said, "Go find Erin!" Erin is a good friend of
mine, and somehow I knew she was there.*

*Then we were all in a condo. Michael was there, lifeless, and
now he was a six-month-old. Everyone was ignoring us. I called
9-1-1. The person on the line said, 'Cut up a cucumber, soak
it in rubbing alcohol, then put it in his mouth to see if he's
dead'—sort of like smelling salts, I guess. I thought, 'How can
I go on if the last vision of Michael is that look of terror under
the wave?'*

*Erin is there now—she said to do CPR after changing my
clothes. I got celery and vodka because I didn't have cucumber
and rubbing alcohol. I prayed, 'Jesus, don't take my baby!' He
stirred, but now he was a little girl with brown hair and eyes.
He opened his eyes and came into my arms. I said, 'Thank you,
Jesus!'"*

In this dream, Bernadette reprises her sense of helplessness and
hopelessness in the face of danger, her feelings of loss and even desire
for death in the face of her divorce, but she is able to call upon inner
resources. She associated her friend Erin with her "spiritual side,"
and her dream prayers with the strength her faith gave her. She
described her skill of "improvising" in the symbol of the vodka-
celery substitution for alcohol-cucumber. Her unconscious was
telling her how to manage her life and in the process, save her
son—who represented also her own childhood self—despite her fear
and escapist longings for care from her husband.

Week by week in rapid succession after this set of dreams, Bernadette
began walking across the Red Sea. She began to think about a

career for herself—she opened her own checking account—she asked William to acknowledge feelings she had about a visitation scheduling conflict. She felt a growing hunger for "something real" in relationships and an increasing recognition that people aren't always what they seem. She confronted a problem with her older brother and exulted, "I found my adult voice!" She asked William and her lawyer to set a date to finalize the divorce. Her feelings of fear and loneliness, her wish for care and escape—these did not change immediately, but she was moving toward her mature and independent adult self and a new life. She was going forward!

Leaps and Forks

When thinking about the way the Red Sea decision plays out in an individual life, I find two metaphors come to mind. The first is a fork in the road, beautifully described in Robert Frost's well-known poem, "The Road Not Taken."[112] The fork in the road, in fact, leads to the second, the leap of faith, a term derived from the work of Søren Kierkekaard, the Danish Christian existentialist philosopher. Both of these images capture an element of the experience of choosing to go forward. Both portray the experience of grappling with the unknown. Both suggest the element of choice, of will. Yet they are very different in mood.

In Frost's poem, the mood is quiet, the decision remembered wistfully. The poet reminisces about a moment of choice, pausing in an autumn-colored forest to consider which fork in the road to take. With the wisdom of hindsight, he concludes,

> Two roads diverged in a wood, and I—
> I took the one less traveled by,
> And that has made all the difference.

---

[112] Robert Frost, p. 219.

Frost's poem captures the sense of the irrevocable that is inherent in a Red Sea decision. The poet is aware that this particular decision will not come again and that it will change his life. He knows that he cannot choose both paths, even as he tries to soften the decision for himself by saying that later he might return to try the road he didn't take. He does not suggest that there is one "right" or "rational" choice, as we so often believe. In fact, he recognizes that his choice, made simply because it appealed to him, fit for him, "has made all the difference" in his life.

Kierkegaard's phrase captures the emotional intensity that is also inherent in a Red Sea decision. A leap of faith is less the choosing of a fork in a road curving through a yellow wood and more the breakneck flinging of oneself across—or into—a dark abyss! It underscores the courage required to face your fears and the grit-your-teeth-and-do-it quality of the moment of choosing.

Choosing to risk something new in the real world or choosing to explore one's inner world—which as we will see inevitably leads one to the other—are leaps of faith. They are forks in a road that will irrevocably change our lives. Consulting the facts and our feelings and then making a decision of the will in the face of our fear is a leap of faith, and it is the decision that we will find has made all the difference. Because the leap of faith is a leap out into what we do not know, and because what we do not know is always the place of what is new, there is no way around it. Because we can only see so far down unknown paths, there is no way around it. "Why do you cry to me? Tell the people to go forward!"

When I stepped across the crevasse high up on Mount Olympus, when Bernadette turned away from her dependence on her ex-husband, when the poet took the road less traveled by, when the Israelites crossed the Red Sea, what awaited us? We were not magically and immediately transported to a state of happily-ever-after. I still had to hike down the mountain. Bernadette still had to build a life for herself. The poet continued his journey through the woods. The Israelites did not find themselves immediately in the Promised Land. Instead, they found themselves wandering in the wilderness. What can we discover about the next step in the process of transformation as we explore that strange and seminal experience?

So, boy, don't you turn back.
Don't you set down on the steps
'Cause you finds it's kinder hard.
Don't you fall now—
Langston Hughes

Chapter Seven:
Wandering in the Wilderness

I walked my dogs on the beach at Half Moon Bay today. It was a glorious autumn day in mid-October: brilliant sunshine, gentle breeze, curling green water, shining sand littered with pebbles and bits of shell. There were a few mothers whose little ones dug in the sand with shovels and pails. There were a few other dogs, too, which thrilled little Fritzy to the tips of his toes—well, paws. It was the sort of day when it would have been wonderful to run, like Fritz, naked on the beach!

Yet, thrilling as it is, naked on the beach is perhaps not so wonderful an experience for everyone at the seashore. Hermit crabs have a brief but risky moment naked on the beach when they must leave behind an old shell and take up residence in a new and roomier one. Those vulnerable steps from the old home to the new must be exhilarating but anxious ones. It reminds me of the stage of the transformative process the Israelites experienced wandering in the wilderness. Their old world was gone, but the new one had not yet come. Freedom and excitement, yes, but also exposure and vulnerability, uncertainty and doubt, high anxiety and defensive maneuvers—all of these thread through that betwixt and between time for hermit crabs, Israelites, and for each of us as we find ourselves beyond our Red Sea decision to go forward.

In the last chapter, we left our heroes in a moment of praise and rejoicing—like Fritzy romping on the beach. Miriam and the women of Israel were playing tambourines, dancing, and singing. Everyone was awed and amazed at their miraculous deliverance from the armies of Egypt and the waters of the Red Sea. They were heady with miracle and freedom! We might imagine Moses watching the celebration . . .

The people are crazy with amazement and with their freedom—their eyes are glowing, their smiles contagious. I find myself smiling with them, glad in their gladness, but my heart is full of foreboding. The fragrance of the lambs grilling over the spits makes my mouth water, but my stomach is queasy, fearing what is to come next. We've seen miracles and wonders. God said he would be present and he has been as good as his word. But now comes a task, if anything, greater than what has come before. Less dramatic maybe, yet far more difficult. We must sustain ourselves, 600,000 strong, in the desert of the Sinai, and for how long?

I know this land well. It is no hospitable place. We must find water. We must eat. We must avoid poisonous creatures and pestilence. We must govern ourselves without the Egyptians to enforce order, to direct our days. We must prepare for battles, perhaps we must fight;. And for how long?

~~~~~~~

The Israelites did not leave Egypt and walk straight to the Promised Land—and this is true of our journeys of transformation as well. The Bible suggests why:

> "It so happened that after Pharaoh released the people, God didn't lead them by the road through the land of the Philistines, which was the shortest route, for God thought, 'If the people encounter war, they'll change their minds and go back to Egypt.'"[113]

Apparently the Israelites had some lessons to learn before they could cope with the challenges they would encounter in taking the Promised Land. The wilderness stage in the journey is a dark and anxious one in which we have left the old behind but the new has not yet come. We need time to practice turning from old ways and exploring new ones, giving up old identities and forging new ones. It's the beating heart of the process of deep transformative change. What can the Exodus story teach us about what must be learned when we, like the children of Israel, find ourselves bewildered and wandering in the wilderness?

The Exodus Story

Bitter Made Sweet: First Lesson of the Wilderness

After celebrating their Red Sea crossing, the Israelites traveled three days into the desert of the Sinai without finding any water. Finally, arriving at an oasis, they were disappointed and angry to find that the water was undrinkable. "That's why they called the place Marah (Bitter)"—the water was bitter, the people were bitter—"The people complained to Moses, 'So what are we supposed to drink?'"[114] Moses'

---

[113] Exodus 13:17
[114] Exodus 15:23-24

fears were already becoming manifest reality, but Moses cried out to God and God provided a solution, the first of many strange and useful things that occurred in the wilderness. "God pointed him to a stick of wood. Moses threw it into the water and the water turned sweet."[115]

The answer to Moses' prayer was not merely fresh water. It was also a tip on survival during the wilderness time: a solution would be found when they asked, when they opened themselves up to something new. Centuries later, Jesus, steeped in the Exodus story of his people, summarized the same principle: "Ask, and it will be given to you; search, and you will find; knock, and the door will be opened for you."[116] That is the first lesson of the wilderness.

This small incident begins the wandering-in-the-wilderness years for Israel, and in it we see a sequence of events that will occur again and again throughout the story. The people become anxious, afraid, unsure—they cope with their anxiety in their old familiar ways (sometimes one might, and the Scripture does, call it "complaining")—Moses asks and opens himself to an answer to the problem facing them, crying out to God—and a new way is revealed, usually providing a very practical solution to their problem as well as lessons on how to survive in the wilderness and ultimately to thrive in life. Remember the still, small voice that Elijah heard on the mountain? It offered a very practical solution to Elijah's problem, too: get Elisha's help, and it taught the important life lesson we discussed earlier—listen within. Let's take a look at the next few episodes in the wilderness period to see how this sequence of events played out again and again.

---

[115] Exodus 15:25
[116] Matthew 7:7, RSV

Quail and Manna: The Second and Third Lessons

Five weeks later, we find the Israelites again upset and anxious—and complaining. This time it's not about water, but food. They were hungry and hungering after the plentiful and familiar foods of Egypt. "Why didn't God let us die in comfort in Egypt where we had lamb stew and all the bread we could eat? You've brought us out into the wilderness to starve us to death, the whole company of Israel!"[117]

It must have been terrifying for the Israelites to see their supplies dwindling after a month and a half in the desert. Their livestock could not reproduce quickly enough to supply so many hungry stomachs. They had no kitchen gardens, no fields with ripening crops. Their only stores of dried figs, herbs, and onions were what they had carried away. Clearly they would have to supplement all of this by living off the land, but the people of Israel did not know how to survive in this unfamiliar land—and, harsh and barren, this land wasn't easy to survive. Nonetheless, we can observe a certain bitter dependency, a slave mentality, as they complained to their leaders: Take care of us! We're not happy, and it's your fault! Do something!

They were afraid of being unable to manage on their own—they were afraid of discomfort, certainly, but also of death. They had longed for freedom—and they had been given their freedom—but had not yet recognized that tremendous and sometimes terrifying responsibility comes with it. It must have begun to be apparent to them, as Moses had already anticipated, that their wilderness sojourn was not going to be a matter of days, but months and perhaps years. Who knew how long? They were afraid—and angry that they were afraid. They complained, blamed, wanted to be taken care of, and demanded assurances and solutions. Again Moses went to

---

[117] Exodus 16:3

God. Again an answer was given. In this case, meat and bread were provided, but not in the way the Israelites expected.

> That evening quail flew in and covered the camp, and in the morning there was a layer of dew all over the camp. When the layer of dew had lifted, there on the wilderness ground was a fine flaky something, fine as frost on the ground. The Israelites took one look and said to one another, *man-hu* (What is it?). They had no idea what it was.
>
> So Moses told them, "It's the bread God has given you to eat." The Israelites named it manna (What is it?). It looked like coriander seed, whitish. And it tasted like a cracker with honey.[118]

As in the bitter-made-sweet solution, this answer provided a practical solution to the serious problem at hand: the need for sustenance in this barren and rocky place. In addition, there was a deeper lesson to be learned. This time when they asked, the answer arrived, but in an unexpected form—quail instead of lamb stew, manna instead of bread. The second lesson the Israelites were shown was that answers, solutions, will indeed come, but they may not be in the form they expected. *"Man-hu?"* they asked, "What is it?" This solution was so new and unexpected that they did not even recognize it! God's creative solution to their problem was resented at first—this was not what they'd ordered. Yet it was exactly what they needed.

The third lesson of the wilderness comes from the fact that this solution to the Israelites' problem, this manna, had a very peculiar quality. They couldn't save it up—they couldn't hoard it. God told the people not to try, but of course some did. They found that on the second day "it got wormy and smelled bad."[119] They had to gather

---

[118] Exodus 16:13-15, 31
[119] Exodus 16:20

manna daily, just as much as they needed, no more but no less. They were being taught to seek what they needed one day at a time. Again, Jesus interprets this lesson later: "Do not worry about tomorrow, for tomorrow will bring worries of its own. Today's trouble is enough for today."[120] One day at a time, sometimes one hour at a time, is all they needed to handle. In wilderness times, that single hour or day can seem an eternity.

Sabbath: A Fourth Lesson

Now, the strange thing was that this one-day-at-a-time rule held true for most of the week, but on the sixth day, the people were to gather twice as much as they needed for that day. Then, on the seventh day, they were *not* to gather, but instead were to rest. On the seventh day, the manna had not turned wormy and did not smell bad. Furthermore, when some of the people went out to gather manna on the seventh day—against the rules—they did not find any at all! The seventh day, the Sabbath, was for rest. So here was a fourth lesson on surviving in the wilderness: even in the face of survival fears, stop working sometimes—rest. There is a rhythm to life: work and rest, push forward and let go, try and stop trying, focus and then don't focus for awhile. Rest is restorative and enables us to work harder and see answers more clearly. In his rendering of the Bible in contemporary language, Eugene Peterson beautifully phrases Jesus' gloss on this lesson:

> "Are you tired? Worn out? Burned out on religion? Come to me. Get away with me and you'll recover your life. I'll show you how to take a real rest. Walk with me and work with me—watch how I do it. Learn the unforced rhythms of grace."[121]

---

[120] Matthew 6:34, RSV
[121] Matthew 11:28-29

Let go and rest sometimes, especially in the wilderness.

Water from the Rock

Again the people moved on, and again they became frustrated and frightened by the lack of drinking water. The parting of the Red Sea waters, the bitter water made sweet, the manna and quail, the pillar of fire and smoke that went before them—all these miracles notwithstanding, they were again angry and afraid. Again they coped by complaining, shifting responsibility, and demanding (or whining for) care. "Why did you take us from Egypt and drag us out here with our children and animals to die of thirst?"[122] This time it was not only Moses they targeted for blame and wheedling manipulation: "Is God here with us, or not?"[123]

Again Moses cried out to God. Again God provided a solution: "Go on out ahead of the people, taking with you some of the elders of Israel. Take the staff you used to strike the Nile. And go. I'm going to be present before you there on the rock at Horeb. You are to strike the rock. Water will gush out of it and the people will drink."[124] Again, the solution provided was practical and amazingly detailed, and again Moses obeyed and the problem was solved. It's interesting to notice, and perhaps identify with, the fact that the Israelites were having trouble holding onto the lessons they were learning. They had just experienced God providing water at Marah, and yet they already needed a review.

Again, beyond meeting the people's practical need, the solution God offered began addressing a deeper difficulty. They had begun to learn how to survive in the wilderness, but the lessons they were learning were also useful strategies for thriving in life beyond the wilderness.

---

[122] Exodus 17:2
[123] Exodus 17:7
[124] Exodus 17:5-6

These surviving and thriving lessons were providing the foundation for a deep transformational shift in an identity that had been so damaged by hundreds of years of slavery. The Israelites might have asked it this way: How, now that we've left the old ways behind, do we find new ones? How do we become a people with a new identity and culture, with independent political, religious, and economic and social systems not of Egypt or of ourselves as slaves in Egypt, but of the true selves God intended us to be? Answers began to be given for these questions of how to create a new identity and of how to structure themselves as an independent people. Here elders, leaders of the people, were brought along to witness the miracle. Political and social leadership must be established if you are going to be an independent society.

A Father-in-Law's Wisdom: The Fifth Lesson

At this point in the journey, it appears that Jethro, the priest of Midian and Moses' father-in-law, had heard rumors about what had been happening with the Israelites. He brought Moses' wife Zipporah and Moses' two sons and came to see for himself. Moses and Jethro chatted and perhaps ate manna and talked over the whole amazing story. The next day, Jethro watched as Moses went about his business as leader of the Israelites. We can imagine Moses glad to show his father-in-law all his responsibility and authority as he sat down to serve as judge for those seeking him out—and there were lots of people seeking him out.

> People were standing before him all day long, from morning to night. When Moses' father-in-law saw all that he was doing for the people, he said, "What's going on here? Why are you doing all this, and all by yourself, letting everybody line up before you from morning to night?"

Moses said to his father-in-law, "Because the people come to me with questions about God. When something comes up, they come to me. I judge between a man and his neighbor, and teach them God's laws and instructions."

Moses' father-in-law said, "This is no way to go about it. You'll burn out and the people right along with you. This is way too much for you—you can't do this alone. Now listen to me. Let me tell you how to do this so that God will be in this with you."[125]

More answers and strategies were now forthcoming, more information on how to become a new people. Jethro suggested some very effective solutions to the problems Moses had been trying to solve: how to teach the people about God, how to institute social and judicial systems based on right and not might. He suggested that Moses serve as an intercessor for the people in bringing their concerns to God and as a teacher of the rules and ways to live. He suggested a system of hierarchically organized political and judicial leadership, with Moses as the primary leader and supreme judge. This hierarchical system of judges would offer individuals the right to appeal what they felt was an unfair judgment—and it would enable Moses to handle far fewer cases, only those that truly needed his ultimate authority. This time Jethro mediated the answer, offering guidance for developing an independent Israelite nation, and preserved Moses from burnout while he was at it. A fifth lesson: when in the wilderness, you don't have to do it all by yourself. Be open to the help that comes—even from an in-law! Use your support system.

So, in the wilderness, there were layers to the lessons that were being learned. First, there were practical solutions to practical problems: the need for water and food for 600,000 people. There were also lessons on how to survive in the wilderness: ask, expect the unexpected when you do, rest, and accept help. These lessons suggested how to

---

[125] Exodus 18:14-19

thrive in life, lessons with wide application for all of life and all of us. Finally, the lessons of the wilderness were specifically tuned to the unique need of the Israelites on their Exodus journey: nurturing a deep shift in their sense of self, of being.

Let's consider this deep shift. The people of Israel were being asked to leave their old slave mentality of bitter dependency, but they were not to become completely self-reliant and wholly autonomous. They were to become adults who could take responsibility but also receive help. They were to become an independent people who could learn, grow, and cooperate with each other and with God. This balance—between taking responsibility for oneself and at the same time being open to what others bring, between independence and dependence—has been called mature dependency or interdependency. It is the new way for Israel and the key both to their new identity and ultimately to their ability to take the Promised Land and settle into it as a people.

The story is not over yet, and the lessons to be learned are not finished. Next comes a very strange sequence of events, yet it follows the same pattern we've been observing in which old ways of coping must be replaced by new ones. It also carries Israel forward toward their new identity as a free and interdependent people.

The Golden Calf: Lesson Six

It had only been three months since the people left Egypt. Witnessing something like a volcanic eruption on the mountain next to which they were camped, the people were afraid and drew back while Moses and Aaron, and then Moses, Aaron, and numerous other leaders, and finally Moses and Joshua, his young aide, climbed the mountain to talk to God.

Up Moses went and down he came to give the people the first version of the Ten Commandments. Up the mountain and down, up and down he went to offer detailed practical advice about handling all kinds of problematic situations: slavery, manslaughter, kidnapping, oxen who gored people, theft, fire damage, sex, gossip, festivals and more. The people said, "Everything God said, we'll do."[126] Up the mountain Moses went a fifth time, and this time he returned with lengthy instructions for new religious rituals, the priesthood, and the place of worship. When it was all planned out, God gave Moses stone tablets to memorialize these instructions. The wilderness period was a time explicitly to work out the implications of Israel's new ways, to structure new ways of being in the world as a people—everything from nutrition and hygiene to social and religious order. Jethro's advice was only a beginning. The biblical books of Exodus, Leviticus, Numbers, and Deuteronomy give detailed plans and careful rules for living and for living together.

Now this last trip up the mountain took a very long time. People started getting scared that they'd lost Moses. They began to feel abandoned and panicky. They were still thinking as slaves. They forgot all about the five lessons they had been taught so far, the new ways. They fell back on their old ways of coping. Instead of interdependency, they fell back into a problematic but very human compromise: they wanted to be taken care of, but they also wanted to control that care.

> When the people realized that Moses was taking forever in coming down off the mountain, they rallied around Aaron and said, "Do something. Make gods for us who will lead us. That Moses, the man who got us out of Egypt—who knows what's happened to him?"[127]

---

[126] Exodus 24:3
[127] Exodus 32:1

Anxiety and coping—this time the Israelites who had witnessed the awful and awe-full wholly otherness of the living God created a god, an idol, something psychologists might call a transitional object, something they could control and so create for themselves the illusion of security. Aaron caved in to the people's pressure and perhaps his own ambition. They melted down their jewelry and made a golden calf.

When Moses came down the mountain to discover this shocking turn of events, he smashed the stone tablets in his fury, confronted Aaron (who passed the buck and evaded—an old way), and forced the people to drink water in which he'd mixed the ash of the smashed and incinerated golden calf. He demanded that people choose which god they served. It all ended with bloodshed by sword and death by plague. The Scripture says that of the more than 600,000 people who left Egypt, three thousand were slain by their kin. Finally, Moses went back up the mountain a sixth and seventh time, alone, to replace the stone tablets of the Ten Commandments and to renew Israel's special relationship with God.

This is a primitive, bloody, and difficult part of the story. God was angry over the people's lapse into old ways, and originally intended to destroy them all and start over with Moses' family alone. Moses begged God for mercy for the people, but then suddenly unleashed his own Shadow fury on them. There was another plague. What was going on? Perhaps this strange incident teaches something about a sixth lesson of the wilderness: old ways of coping are not just unattractive—they can be dangerous. They can destroy the very things they are designed to secure. How is this so?

God's anger and Moses' fury are understandable. The children of Israel, like all children, were not always winsome. They whined, complained, wheedled, cajoled, manipulated, quarreled, bitched, moaned, and tried to control things so they could have their own way. This is certainly not attractive, but is it dangerous? Did it deserve such immoderate punishment? What happens when children whine, complain, wheedle; when they try to control things and get their own way? They may well get what they want, but whether they do or not, by going about it in these ways they end up undercutting their relationships and their sense of respect and admiration for themselves. They get their own way and lose what they really need—love, security, and self-esteem.

This difficult incident demonstrates a sort of self-fulfilling prophecy in which the very thing the Israelites were trying to avoid is what they got—and the very thing they were trying to get is what they destroyed. In trying to create safety, to control life by means of the golden calf, they ended up losing their lives altogether. Jesus said: "Self-help is no help at all. Self-sacrifice is the way, my way, to finding yourself, your true self. What kind of deal is it to get everything you want but lose yourself? What could you ever trade your soul for?"[128] So again, the sixth lesson of the wilderness: the old ways may be familiar and easy, but they are binding and dangerous. Hold to the new ways and walk into freedom.

What happened next taught a seventh and final lesson on surviving and thriving both in the wilderness and in life. Moses had heard the voice of God from the burning bush. He had seen signs and wonders performed by God, learned lessons and been given the Ten Commandments by God. He now wished to see God face to face.

God's Face and God's Name: the Seventh Lesson

On Moses' seventh trip up the mountain, he asked that he might see God's glory and God agreed: "I will make my Goodness pass right in front of you; I'll call out the name, God, right before you.

---

[128] Matthew 16:25

But you may not see my face. No one can see me and live."[129]
Now God—whose name during the time of the plagues was I-Am-
Present—intended to reveal more of himself. Hiding Moses in the
cleft of a rock, God passed by him and called out his name:

> "God, God, a God of mercy and grace, endlessly patient—so
> much love, so deeply true—loyal in love for a thousand
> generations, forgiving iniquity, rebellion, and sin. Still,
> he doesn't ignore sin. He holds sons and grandsons
> responsible for a father's sins to the third and even fourth
> generation."[130]

The seventh lesson of the wilderness was simply this: God's name—
that is, a description of God's essential being and therefore what
is ultimately the most real of all realities and the core nature of
nature—is mercy and grace, patience and love, truth and justice. Any
new way must respond to reality and, like a good hypothesis, is better
the more it does. Old ways do not serve and are finally destructive
because they do not respond to reality, and in fact, even prevent us
from seeing it well. The Israelites' new ways aligned with what was
ultimately more real—the old ways did not. Interdependency aligns
with it—a bitter dependency that avoids responsibility while it tries
to control things anyway does not.

In the seventh lesson, God spoke his name but didn't show his face.
This is a pair of powerful metaphors and contains a warning meant
to deepen Moses' humility as well as our own. The warning: we can
know something about the nature of Ultimate Reality, but we can
only know it as mediated by symbols—as Paul said, "We don't yet see
things clearly. We're squinting in a fog, peering through a mist."[131]
A Buddhist koan makes the same distinction when it warns us not

---

[129] Exodus 33:19-20
[130] Exodus 34:6-7
[131] I Corinthians 13:12

to mistake the finger pointing to the moon for the moon itself. We must be careful not to mistake the idea or image for the reality itself. Ultimate Reality, that is God's essential being, goes beyond our ability to do more than glimpse it, point toward it, know something about it. Joseph Campbell spoke to this truth when he said that we use metaphors, poetry, and myth "because the ultimate cannot be put into words. It is beyond words, beyond images . . . . Mythology pitches the mind . . . to what can be known but not told."[132] We may know God's name, but we may not see God's face and live.

This may be a place to note the value of the many metaphors used to describe God. Throughout the book you may have noticed that I have used the masculine pronoun when referring to God. This is in keeping with most biblical usage and my own habit of thought, but does not mean that I believe that God is male. God transcends masculinity and femininity. Father, Mother, Rock, Hiding Place, Joy, Source, Light, Wind, Energy, the Universe—each are metaphors that point to an aspect of God, though God transcends any metaphor that we might use. Any single metaphor necessarily limits our understanding of the truest, deepest reality of God—the Thou of Martin Buber,[133] the God who is beyond the God of theism and the Ultimate Concern of Paul Tillich,[134] the Is-ness of the Buddhists. The personhood of God—God as one who knows and loves and chooses to act—is an aspect of God that I feel is lost, at least in English, in the use of the neuter pronoun "it" and even in a contraction like "he/ she." It is impossible to read the story of the Exodus or the teaching of Jesus without coming face to face, so to speak, with an awareness of God's personhood. I believe it is the great contribution of the Judeo-Christian faiths to the world.

---

[132] Joseph Campbell with Bill Moyers, *The Power of Myth*, ed. Betty Sue Flowers (New York: Doubleday, 1988), p. 161.

[133] See Martin Buber, *I and Thou*, first published in 1937.

[134] See, for example, Paul Tillich's *Dynamics of Faith*, originally published in 1957.

So, the seventh lesson of the wilderness time can be discerned in the mysterious and mystical passage with which this part of the Exodus story ends. It is this: the deepest nature of reality—the name of God, I-Am-Present, and the truth that lies behind every metaphor—is mercy and grace, endless patience and love, truth and justice. The new ways align with him; the old ways do not. When anxiety and fear come, hold to him. When you have had the courage to leave the old enslaving place behind, hold to him. When you reach the Promised Land, hold to him—in fact, you won't reach the Promised Land otherwise, but hold to your understanding of him humbly, as necessarily a partial revelation of Ultimate Reality. We may know his name, but we cannot see his face and live.

The prophet Micah summarized this seventh lesson several centuries later when he wrote:

> He has shown you, O mortal, what is good;
> and what does the Lord require of you
>> but to do justice,
>> and to love kindness,
>> and to walk humbly with your God?[135]

When Moses experienced this seventh lesson and revelation, when he came down the mountain for the seventh time, the teller of the Exodus story says: "his face glowed."[136] Any encounter with God, with what is finally most real, is very, very transformative, and any transformation enables us better to live in adaptive response to the immediate realities of our lives and in tune with the nature of Ultimate Reality, with mercy and grace, patience and love, truth and justice.

---

[135] Micah 6:8, NRSV
[136] Exodus 34:29

Being afraid—coping in the old ways—searching and opening—
finding an answer and a new way: this is the pattern that we see
repeat itself as the Israelites walked through the wilderness of the
Sinai. What purpose does this wandering in the wilderness period
serve on a transformative journey? How does psychology expand our
understanding of and toleration for this kind of experience when it
happens in our own lives?

Adaptation

Wandering in the wilderness is a time when we are changing our
existing conception of the world and ourselves in it—and perhaps
of the nature of Ultimate Reality as well. Jean Piaget, considered
the founding father of modern developmental psychology, was a
Swiss biologist, philosopher, and psychologist who studied this very
process in children, largely through minute observation of his own
three children.

> For most parents, when a toddler knocks down a set of
> blocks it means another mess to clean up; for Piaget it was a
> valuable clue as to how the human mind reasons. He would
> ask: Did the child knock the blocks down in any particular
> order? According to size? Shape? Color? Did he laugh while
> he was doing it? From such observations, Piaget traced the
> origins of mental growth through early childhood.[137]

Piaget believed that reasoning based on experience is the fundamental
building block of intelligence. Though the physical substrate of
intelligence—the structure of the brain and the sensory organs—
is biologically determined, the child's capacity to reason and
understand develops as he grows. Therefore, he must continually

---

[137] Dorothy G. Singer & Tracey A. Revenson, *A Piaget Primer: How a Child Thinks*
(New York: Penguin Books, 1978, 1996), p. 7.

revise and reorganize his understanding of the world as he develops. Piaget called this process of revising and reorganizing "adaptation." "Initially, a child attempts to understand a new experience by applying old solutions . . . when this doesn't work the child is forced to change his existing conception of the world in order to interpret the experience."[138]

Adaptation is a two-step process. The first step, assimilation, involves absorbing new information and fitting it into an idea or mental structure—something Piaget called a "schema"—which we already have. The playroom chair, the dining room chair, the kitchen stool, and the picnic bench all fit the same flat-surfaced-thing-with-legs-that-you-sit-on schema. Chalk, pencils, crayons, and pens all fit the same thin-cylinder-thing-that-you-make-marks-with-and-mother-thinks-you're-great schema.

The second step, accommodation, occurs when we encounter something that doesn't fit into a pre-existing mental structure. Then we have to revise our schemas to fit the new information. A table is like a chair, but you don't sit on the table . . . usually. Mom thinks it's great when I draw, but when I draw on the walls she is furious—always.

Adaptation is essentially a process of becoming more and more in tune with reality, both immediate and physical as well as ultimate and metaphysical. When old solutions have failed and we must accommodate new information in order to adapt, we may temporarily be confused and disoriented. It is like wandering in the wilderness. Like the hermit crab, we have left the old, too-small shell behind and are still finding our way into the new shell that better fits the realities we are discovering. Like the Israelites, we have left Egypt but have not yet taken the Promised Land.

---

[138] Ibid. p. 15.

Piaget's theory of adaptation is a cognitive learning theory—the processes he observed are intellectual reasoning processes, but human beings are also emotional creatures whose lives depend on social interactions with each other. This fact can add a speed bump, a barrier, to the accommodation process, especially when it comes to the kinds of old learning that need revising—as we saw when safety becomes slavery.

Psychodynamic therapists call these speed bumps "psychological defenses" while more cognitively-oriented therapists call them "coping strategies." A large part of any transformative journey requires getting over these speed bumps, or, to use a different metaphor, getting past the guard at the gate of Piaget's adaptation process. All psychotherapies and spiritual practices aim to facilitate this gate-crashing. Let's consider how those speed bumps or gates, psychological defenses or coping strategies, operate in more detail.

Everyone has characteristic patterns of defenses or coping strategies—those brilliant childhood solutions to very real problems. Those patterns form the essence of our unique personality structure or style.[139] When we rigidly and compulsively cope with anything and everything that comes our way using our learned defenses, we are not adapting well to the realities we confront as adults. When we cope in characteristic ways but can also flexibly modify our choices as situations call for something else, we are adaptive and healthy. We function better in the real world, here and now.

For example, if I typically cope by avoiding confrontation, I may be very well liked and get along in many situations—until I am given responsibility for managing people, or I begin to feel unsafe in my marriage, or my child needs better boundaries. Then I may find that my ways of coping don't help and may even contribute to the problems

---

[139] I give credit to René Tillich, Ph.D., for teaching me the tremendous clinical value of understanding personality style.

I face. There are many situations in which avoiding confrontation may be just the right approach, but there will be situations in which it is exactly the wrong approach, exacerbating problems instead of solving them. Of course, there are other approaches that sometimes work and sometimes don't. We can get organized, or close down and go to sleep, or create drama to hide and get attention at the same time, or worry about appearances, or believe that the best defense is a good offense. Our defenses operate from pre-existing schemata that may or may not correspond closely with the actual circumstances, the realities, at hand.

Some defensive strategies actually operate to change our ability even to recognize reality or to rightly value what we know. For example, perhaps we learned that our perceptions were called wrong or considered threatening by those we loved. We can use substances to submerge our perceptions and reactions—directly ingested or internally produced. Drugs, alcohol, food, exercise, or sex help us numb out and disengage or change our mood. We can deny realities that don't fit our schema or our wishes, not seeing and therefore not knowing, or we can know but oddly not feel anything. We can say, "I don't care" or minimize the importance of something that is important. We can limit our focus to details until we can't see the forest for the trees, or simply find ourselves far away from the present place and time, sometimes actually and physically, but usually mentally.

Other defenses are designed to manage our awareness of disturbing realities as well, but operate more in the interpersonal sphere. Projection protects us from what we cannot confront within ourselves because we believe it's out there in someone else. If we cannot deal with our own inadequacy or smallness, we can feel adequate and big if someone else is small. If we cannot deal with our own anger, we can feel calm when someone else becomes angry. If we cannot deal with our own wish for freedom and play, we can remain responsible but marry a charming player, and if we are afraid of using our own power, we can find someone comfortable with using theirs.

The slave mentality of the children of Israel involved just this sort of coping strategy. They projected their own power and responsibility onto Moses and God, feeling vulnerable and needy when they actually could take responsibility—then engaged in controlling and manipulating to compensate for it. They couldn't see their own responsibility, couldn't feel their own power when they had it. As a result, they weren't able to be appropriately dependent *or* independent.

The Serenity Prayer approaches this problem beautifully:

> God, grant me the serenity to accept the things I cannot change,
> the courage to change the things I can,
> and the wisdom to know the difference. [140]

In other words, "God, undo my defenses and give me grace to cope with reality!"

The Shadow within—Moses' burning bush—and the plagues of external circumstances break down the gates of our defensiveness. We find that our old ways of coping are inadequate. If we decide to leave Egypt, to cross the Red Sea and go forward, we are beginning to give up our old defensive strategies and to break into the chain of hurt and damage they forge. We risk doing something differently in the world. When we give up our old defensive strategies, we begin to confront realities we have avoided, to begin to know. Beginning to know means that Piaget's process of adaptation can take place, but it also means that we will feel feelings of exposure and uncertainty— we will be wandering in the wilderness—as we forge a new and

---

[140] Often attributed to Reinhold Niebuhr, great twentieth century theologian, this prayer became widely circulated when adopted by Alcoholics Anonymous.

healthier relationship with reality. A client put it well just yesterday: "Things you thought were foundational truths were not!"

The lessons of the wilderness help us when we have risked facing the knowledge we didn't want to know and the feelings of anxiety or vulnerability, or power or anger that we didn't want to feel. The lessons of the wilderness help us during times of uncertainty and insecurity as we better adapt to reality and learn to cope in new ways. We can appropriate these lessons for ourselves:

1. Answers will come if we open ourselves to them.
2. Answers, however, may not come in the form we expect.
3. Take it one day at a time—sometimes one hour at a time.
4. Don't forget to stop working and rest.
5. Don't try to do it alone—be open to receive the help others give.
6. Old ways of coping are not just unattractive—they are often dangerous. They can destroy the very things they are designed to secure, and they prevent us from opening to new realities we have not recognized. Hold to the new ways.
7. Remember that God's names—descriptions of his being and therefore of that which is ultimately most real—are God I-Am-Present and God, God, a God of mercy and grace, endlessly patient—so much love, so deeply true—loyal in love for a thousand generations, forgiving iniquity, rebellion, and sin. New ways respond to what is real, and so come more and more to resemble what is most real, what is most like him.

Being afraid—coping in the old ways—searching and opening—finding an answer and a new way; this is the pattern that we see repeated as the Israelites found their way through the wilderness of the Sinai. The process of adaptation that begins when we get over the speed bumps and past the guard at the gate of our old defensive patterns helps explain what is happening as we wander in the wilderness. What does it look like when it comes to someone's life? How does one person's wandering affect their loved ones? Let's turn to my clients, Brooke and Matthew, to explore these questions.

The Damsel in Distress

"I'm diving in. You came very highly recommended." With the first two sentences she said in our very first therapy session, Brooke communicated the essence of her personality and interpersonal style. James Bibb, Ph.D., helped me to see the importance of my patient's initial moments in therapy. He said, "In the first five minutes of the first therapy session, our patients tell us everything we need to know, but it takes time for us to understand those first five minutes!" So, in her first five minutes Brooke showed me how she closed her eyes and jumped fully into friendships. Then she worked hard to make her friends feel wonderful about themselves, just as she was making me feel wonderful about my (highly recommended) self! This style had undergirded her marriage as well. She and her husband had a passionate, fairytale romance in which he was the rescuing hero and "peace-keeper" and she was the grateful and loving damsel-in-distress who was "emotionally honest," intense, and engaging . . . if a little battered and psychologically bruised.

It all sounded pretty good. What problems could there be? Yet, she had been in therapy for years, was taking antidepressants, woke at night torturing herself over things she had done and said at dinner parties, felt useless and worse than a burden to her husband and loved ones. More, she and her husband could fight with such rapidity and intensity that it was like watching a professional game of ping-pong.

Her coping strategies—jumping into relationships with nothing held back, projecting all sorts of good things onto the other, leaving herself all the bad—were taking a toll. With her eyes closed to reality as she jumped in, she couldn't navigate the reality of the flawed and complexly motivated human beings she loved. She gave all and expected all and was crushed when someone let her down—then turned all her disappointment and anger on herself. She ended up depressed and incapacitated, ashamed and self-flagellating. How were these strategies her childhood solutions to problems?

Childhood Solutions, Adult Problems

Brooke's childhood was chaotic. Her father was a professional gambler, her mother drug—and alcohol-addicted, and in and out of rehab and mental hospitals. She and her little brother spent years in foster care after her parents' divorce and before her new stepmother brought them home. "The women" in her mother's family—her grandmother, mother, aunt, and female cousins—were competitive and jealous, especially about attracting men. How did this sensitive and beautiful little girl cope? She loved—everyone but herself. If there was a problem, it was her fault. A strange inversion occurred: in her mind, others were all good and she was all bad. They were in and she was outside, the little match girl of Hans Christian Anderson's fairytale, trying to get in. They felt great about themselves, briefly, but she felt horrible about herself most of the time. Still, she had a family.

All of this came to a head shortly after we began therapy. Gifted, intelligent, with a flair for the dramatic and a passion for good causes, she was asked to lead the annual stewardship drive at her church. She was thrilled and dove right in with no holds barred—how else? For months she planned and scheduled and gathered connections. It all came to a head with a huge public event: gorgeously executed, thrillingly attended by the entire congregation, and hugely financially successful.

It all sounded pretty good. What problems could there be? But even as compliments still hung in the air, letters of complaint were sent, friends began to gossip, and the community became divided over whether their church should take this fabulous approach to fundraising. The competitiveness and jealousy of "the women" with their indirect communication and behind-the-back coalitions had become a present day reality. The church's elephants-in-the-room, as Alcoholics Anonymous might describe it, woke up and began charging around wrecking havoc. Brooke was crushed beyond crushed. Her husband tried to rescue her, pointing out her own contributions to the problem, her misperceptions of social realities, and her frightening moods. She felt undercut and misunderstood. They argued, and their marriage became a battleground as old elephants began charging around in their house, too.

Brooke's old ways of coping, her safety-become-slavery, had been broken into by depression within and the external plague of the church's competing internal coalitions. She had to choose, a Red Sea decision, to begin to see realities she didn't want to see and to undo the projections of all-good that she didn't want to acknowledge. Slowly and painfully, she began to choose and to enter Piaget's process of adaptation, the wilderness.

The Woman in the Wilderness

The result of this courageous choice was not an immediate step into the Promised Land. Far from it. Things got worse. She became more depressed, even suicidal. Her marriage became stressed to the point that both Matthew and Brooke feared it would end. Brooke was in the heart of the wilderness experience. She said, "Everything

I thought I knew about my life and myself is gone! I don't know who I am!"

To contain this depression, we began to meet together twice a week. She updated her medications with her psychiatrist. Each session we struggled to find the hope she didn't have, to find a way through the darkness. During the hour, she began to see what was real and to feel healthy and appropriate feelings about those realities, past and present—but she could not hold onto it. I suggested that after therapy sessions she take some time to write down statements she had felt were true while we were talking—a truth journal—that she could review when the darkness felt overwhelming. Finally, there came a turning point, a session in which a guided active imagination exercise—like the one with Sylvie in chapter four—dominated the hour.

"There's so much self-loathing!" she said.

"What is the self-loathing like?" I asked. I was thinking that trying to reason her out of these feelings wasn't working—maybe we could go deeper into them.

"It's like a giant gaping hole I'm falling into. Everyone who knows me thinks so. I'm a mess, a wreck, a victim. Please, God, don't let me fall in!"

"Can you bring someone into the scene with you?"

"You and Matthew. We're all looking amazed at how deep and scary the hole is. You and Matthew are thinking that it's as bad as it is and I'm still here."

"Shall we jump in?" I challenged.

"I don't want him to go with us. We jump. I'm screaming. My eyes are closed . . . Now there's nothing else. Matthew is saying, 'Where did they go? I'm scared! I'm alone!'"

"You lost yourself for Matthew?"

"Yes, it seems more important. I needed to save him by my going. He's got his life the way he wants it, and I'm just a bummer."

"I want you to go back to the scene in your imagination," I said. I wanted to bring her back in imagination to what had seemed most emotionally alive. "Can you bring light into the hole?"

"The hole . . . it's more like a wound, a bullet hole! It's worse than I thought. It's more disgusting . . . and fresh. It's embarrassing! Hideous!"

"Where is the hole now? Can you help me see it with you?"

"My chest . . . it's huge, most of my chest is a big, deep wound." She was crying now.

"Can you bring someone to look at it? What do you see in their face?"

"Jesus. I see compassion. Love. He's so sad."

"And what is happening with the wound in your chest?"

"My thought is: stay open so light can touch all of it. But I don't like it!"

Matthew began the next month by saying, "Brooke seems to have changed a bit . . . but I'm wary." Brooke herself felt the need to become "a hermit," to withdraw from most of her social community—though "I so badly want a friend!" She also began to see her relationship with Matthew differently, wrestling with "the idea of our mythic romance; that there is something unhealthy about not being able to see the dark side" but fearing his reaction if "I'm not the way I used to be with him, just all over him!" I told her about the wilderness time for the children of Israel. Together we walked one day at a time, opening ourselves for answers. Brooke hung on.

Over the next several months, she continued to withdraw from the world, cocooning in her home and with her family. She continued to wrestle with her marriage, feeling that her husband would not accept anything but happiness from her. Like Cindy and Josh, she felt, "It's like I need to be happy in order for him to be happy!" I encouraged her to hold to her path, trusting that he would also find his, and tolerating the destabilization of both her internal intrapsychic system and the couple's marital system.

Slowly, she began to see, to act, and to feel differently. Slowly she began to discover her new ways. She found herself worrying less about what other people thought of her. She found herself discovering her own power and strength. She began to see Matthew differently, "I have a more complete and realistic picture of Matthew! When I was in my worshipping mode, everything he did was fabulous. I've realized he's fragile in some ways. He's a really good human being, always—but real." The next week, she happily reported on a dinner party, "I didn't wake up in the middle of the night and feel bad. I didn't worry about every word I said. I feel like there's been some part of me being restored."

"I'm reminded of your image of the wound and Jesus' compassion and healing light."

"Yes," Brooke replied. "Healed and scarred over, and as I come out of the wilderness, I feel more grounded in myself. It's like a miracle."

As Brooke began to give up old ways for new ones, her husband found himself challenged to change, too. A new CEO, Matthew was at the apex of his career. He was very successful, on top of the world, and on the covers of magazines. It was hard for him to believe that any of the couple's problems had anything to do with him, but as Brooke became more grounded and firm in herself, his old patterns began to be challenged. He said, "This therapy stuff . . . I started a process, but now it's uncomfortable, making me unstabilized. I have to finish, but I'm not totally engaging it. But it's engaging me!"

Matthew was being prodded out of his own Egypt, reluctantly, dragged toward the Red Sea and into the wilderness by his love for his wife and the movement toward wholeness that stirred within his own psyche. He was beginning to feel uncomfortable, "unstabilized." Meanwhile, Brooke was becoming stronger, their marriage happier and more relaxed. All the kids were flourishing in new ways. He began to understand that his rescuing Brooke was actually disrespectful to her, triggering her insecurities as well as protecting his own. He began to explore the wounds and triggers that he brought to their relationship himself.

The couple was suffering a sea-change, becoming something rich and strange. Though it began with Brooke's passionate need and equally passionate courage, it was radiating outward in brand-new ways into the larger world for Matthew, their children, his company, their church and community. They were on the move, her journey having provoked his.

Last week, Brooke came to therapy profoundly moved by her reading of a passage in Robert Johnson's memoir. She had begun to reverse the process that began as her childhood solution to problems, that of giving all the good to the other and taking all the weakness, brokenness, and hurt to herself. Johnson's words captured her own journey and new awareness.

Soul work, or inner work, takes place when something moves from the unconscious, where it began, into conscious awareness. The path is never straight and neat inside oneself, as if you could go to a library and do all your inner work there . . . . If it's your gold—your soul—that is coming to consciousness, your first inkling of such a deep internal change will likely be that someone else begins to glow for you. It is your gold, but you see it in someone else; you are putting the alchemical gold on that person . . . .

To exchange a love for another person based on one's own gold for an appreciation of the other's true being is a sublime evolution. One stops seeing a reflection of oneself and, instead, sees the reality of the other person. Reality is always far nobler than any projection.[141]

No Crystal Stair

The work of the wilderness is to forge a strong and resilient link to new ways of being in the world. That means it is the process of becoming robustly aware, of getting past defenses; letting go of denial and taking back projections, good and bad, darkness and gold. That means it is the process of accommodating to realities that we have been avoiding, especially to what is most real: mercy and grace, patience and love, truth and justice—the name of God whose face we cannot yet see. It is thrilling to be free of Egypt. In Cindy's words as she began her wilderness journey, "There's an aspect of excitement in the opportunity. It's like there's a blank canvas and you don't really know what you're painting, but you're doing it and

---

[141] Robert Johnson, *Balancing Heaven and Earth* as previously cited, p. 62-64. For a more elaborate discussion of this projection process in romantic love, see his book, *We: Understanding the Psychology of Romantic Love* (New York: HarperCollins Publishers, 1983). He uses the medieval myth of Tristan and Iseult to trace the dynamics of romantic love both in western culture and in our individual psyches.

you're excited to see what it will be. It's so engaging, it pulls you forward." At the same time, as Matthew said: "I started a process, but now it's uncomfortable, making me unstabilized. I have to finish, but I'm not totally engaging it. But it's engaging me!" Thrilling freedom, excitement, engagement, at the same time vulnerability and anxious uncertainty—the wilderness is "uncomfortable" and inevitably "unstabilizing."

Discussing the transformative journey of the Exodus with another client recently, she asked, "Where am I in the process, do you think?" We both decided she was, in fact, in the wilderness phase. As we thought about it, she made a beautiful observation. She said, "The wilderness . . . I think of it as a forest, not a desert. When you are in the forest at night, you can't see where you are going, it's so dark, but if you look up, you can see the path." To be out in the forest at night can be a thrilling but also an anxious experience. The forest at night has a darkness that we who live in cities rarely know, but the black silhouettes of trees outline a starry path in the night sky. Look up. Her unconscious had chosen the perfect metaphor to describe her own lesson of the wilderness: Look up!

The wilderness lessons show us how to survive and thrive on the path of transformation. If finding our internal Moses involves listening within, moving through the wilderness means looking up and reaching out. That is the essential truth of the seven lessons of the wilderness. Look up and reach out: open yourself to answers and be open when answers aren't what you expect. Take it one day at a time. Take time to rest. Accept what help comes. Remember that the old ways "protect" us from reality, and in so doing limit our ability to receive what is beyond ourselves. Let go of them and hold to the new ways. Look up and reach out to God I-Am-Present—to God, God, a God of mercy and grace, endlessly patient—so much love, so deeply true—loyal in love for a thousand generations, forgiving iniquity, rebellion, and sin.

What does that mean in a practical way? It means looking up from the concerns and problems that preoccupy us so that we may reach out for a larger perspective, for more reality, for the answers that will surely come. It means embracing the present moment, practicing gratitude in the face of fear, scarcity, or threat. It means doing whatever enables us to embrace this moment and that larger perspective in the course of our daily lives and in the course of this very day—journaling about a dream, sitting in silent meditation, having a cup of tea with a friend or a temper tantrum with God, or romping on the beach with a small, black Miniature Schnauzer.

Langston Hughes wrote a beautiful and powerful poem in the voice of someone who also knew the wilderness and had learned its lessons. If you are in a wilderness time, let her speak to you.

Mother to Son

Well, son, I'll tell you:
Life for me ain't been no crystal stair.
It's had tacks in it,
And splinters,
And boards torn up,
And places with no carpet on the floor—
Bare.
But all the time
I'se been a-climbin' on,
And reachin' landin's,
And turnin' corners,
And sometimes goin' in the dark
Where there ain't been no light.
So, boy, don't you turn back.
Don't you set down on the steps
'Cause you finds it's kinder hard.

Don't you fall now—
For I'se still goin', honey,
I'se still climbin',
And life for me ain't been no crystal stair. [142]

When you are in the wilderness, "goin' in the dark where there ain't been no light," look up, reach out, hold on. Look up for the path silhouetted against the stars. Reach out for the help that will come. Hold on. You aren't alone. "For I'se still goin', honey, I'se still climbin', and life for me ain't been no crystal stair."

As we climb and wander, it seems as though the wilderness time will never end. Then suddenly, we find ourselves camped beside the river Jordan, ready to move into the next stage of the transformative journey. Suddenly, we are given an opportunity to move into the Promised Land. Let's explore what that meant for Israel and what it could mean for us as we move forward in our own transformative journeys.

---

[142] Langston Hughes and Arna Bontemps, eds. *The Poetry of the Negro: 1746-1970*, (Garden City, New York: Anchor Press/Doubleday & Co., 1949, 1970), p. 186.

. . . Much will be gained if we succeed in transforming
your hysterical misery into common unhappiness.
With a mental life that has been restored to health
you will be better armed against that unhappiness.
Sigmund Freud

Chapter Eight:
Taking the Promised Land

The taking of the Promised Land is the last chapter in the Exodus story and the first chapter in the story of Israel as a nation. It is less an arrival than a conquest, less a place of security and safety than an opportunity for a freer and fuller becoming. A shift had taken place in the wilderness, a shift of identity, of lessons learned, and of new ways of coping and being. Now the children of Israel were on the move—therapists say "unstuck"—and ready to move forward in a new way. At a similar point, a thoughtful client put it this way: "I went through a shift . . . some deep grief . . . it's a mystery how it all happens. I'm in a vulnerable and strong and willing place—yes, that's it, a willing place."

Let's observe the Israelites as they move out into the Promised Land. We'll see them first in a sort of false start—a premature effort to move out of the wilderness. Then let's watch when they have made that mysterious shift to the vulnerable and strong and willing place my patient described. And finally, let's consider what arriving in the Promised Land actually meant for them.

The Exodus Story

During the second year in the wilderness, Moses chose twelve spies—"all of them were leaders in Israel, one from each tribe"[143]—to scout out the land of Canaan, the Promised Land. They went throughout the countryside from the north to the southern borders, across the Jordan River to the Mediterranean Sea. After forty days (in Scripture "forty" means a good, long time), they returned carrying fruits of the land: pomegranates, figs, and a huge cluster of grapes—ambrosia to a people two years in the desert.

They reported that the land was indeed good, fertile and rich, but the people who lived there were strong and the cities fortified. "We scouted out the land from one end to the other—it's a land that swallows people whole. Everybody we saw was huge . . . Alongside them we felt like grasshoppers. And they looked down on us as if we were grasshoppers."[144] Ten of the scouts were afraid and felt defeated before they started. They said, "We can't do it!"

Caleb, one of the twelve, disagreed. He said, "Let's go up and take the land—now. We can do it."[145] He stood against a tidal wave of mob hysteria. The people were panicked, terrified, angry. Again they rebelled against Moses and Aaron. Again they complained against God, and again they wanted to turn tail and run back to Egypt. Joshua, also one of the scouts, joined Caleb. The two men shouted out over the hubbub, calling the people back to the lessons of the wilderness. "Don't rebel against God! And don't be afraid of those

---

[143] Numbers 13:2
[144] Numbers 13:33
[145] Numbers 13:30

people. Why, we'll have them for lunch! They have no protection and God is on our side. Don't be afraid of them!"¹⁴⁶ But the people were on the verge of stoning Joshua and Caleb to death.

At this intense moment, a mysterious and dramatic thing occurred. "The bright Glory of God appeared at the Tent of Meeting. Every Israelite saw it. God said to Moses, 'How long will these people treat me like dirt?'"¹⁴⁷ Everyone stopped. God's decree underscored a simple truth: until you learn the lessons of the wilderness, until the new ways of coping become second nature to you, you will not—you cannot—take the Promised Land. In fact, all Israelites who were of mature fighting age, all but Joshua and Caleb, would die in the wilderness while a new generation—one for whom the slave mentality of Egypt was a distant memory—grew up. What might have been two years of transition and transit became forty years of wandering. The lessons of the wilderness—lessons that would enable the Israelites to take and possess the new land—needed more time to mature. The Israelites had crossed the Red Sea, but they did not yet know themselves as a people who could claim their promised and longed for heritage, their new identity.

So they continued to wander and to cycle through the same lessons: Look up. Reach out. Hold on. The old ways are unattractive—and even destructive. New ways respond to our particular realities and to what is Ultimate Reality: God I-Am-Present, God whose name is mercy and grace, patience and love, truth and justice. Courageously choose the new ways. As the Israelites wandered through those forty years in the wilderness, they began to have encounters—and battles—with other peoples on the way. They got practical experience in applying the lessons they were learning, in their new skills of faith and courage, in their new interdependency and identity.

---

¹⁴⁶ Numbers 14:7-8
¹⁴⁷ Numbers 14:10-11

The years passed in this way until Moses was very old (Scripture says 120 years old).[148] He had been barred from entering the Promised Land by his own lapse away from the new ways.[149] Joshua had been named Moses' successor by God. With a sweeping vision of the land given to Israel by God, Moses blessed the tribes and charged them to remain true to what they had learned of themselves and of God in the wilderness. Then he climbed Mount Nebo to look out over Jericho.

Ahh, these old bones are heavy, the muscles failing in their strength. And I am weary, body and soul. Zipporah is gone. Miriam is gone. Aaron gone. So many whom I have loved are gone now. The people I led out of Egypt, almost all gone. Their sons and daughters, their grandsons and granddaughters follow Joshua now. It is good. Joshua is like a son to me and in some ways, closer than my own sons. Joshua is one who knows you, God of Abraham, Isaac, and Jacob—God I-Am-Present. Joshua can carry the burden of leadership, and I am glad to put it down.

I can see the green land of the Promise stretching out past the sinuous blue path of the Jordan River. A good land. I wish that I could be with my people as they consummate this long wilderness journey and enter the new land, but I may not. I am still ashamed of my anger, how it flared out yet again by the waters of Meribah. I struck the rock in my anger, sick of their complaining, disgusted by their constant disrespect and rebellion against my leadership. But it was against you, you only that they sinned, and my anger did no good. So many years and still sometimes the old anger flashes out like searing lightening, like a striking snake.

---

[148] Numbers 34:7

[149] See the story in Numbers 20 for an explanation of this lapse. It seems that Moses did not follow God's instructions, instead angrily dramatizing another water-from-the-rock miracle in perhaps a self-aggrandizing or self-justifying way. He must have failed, as a leader, to show the people the God whose name he heard though he could not see his face.

The sun is going down, sinking into the great sea that lies beyond the Jordan and beyond the land of Canaan. The sky is flushing pink. The light is getting dim. Night is coming on, the cold, hard night of the desert. It will be even colder and harder on this rocky mountaintop. Perhaps it will be my last sunset, my last night.

The colors are brightening, and brighter still. How odd. I would have thought they should be fading by now, but the sky is bright with red and purple, the color of ripe pomegranates and grapes—shot through with gold like Pharaoh's collar. It's strange . . . it is brighter now and yet brighter . . . O my God, my God, I see your face!

~~~~~~~

"The people wept for Moses in the plains of Moab thirty days . . . . No prophet has risen since in Israel like Moses, whom God knew face-to-face. Never since has there been anything like the signs and miracle-wonders that God sent him to do in Egypt . . . nothing to compare with . . . all the great and terrible things Moses did as every eye in Israel watched."[150] Though Moses did not enter the land of Canaan with the people of Israel, I think we would be safe in believing that he did cross into the most promised of lands, one in which we see God's face and live.

Then God spoke to Joshua:

> "Moses my servant is dead. Get going. Cross this Jordan River, you and all the people. Cross to the country I'm giving to the People of Israel. In the same way I was with Moses, I'll be with you. I won't give up on you; I won't leave you. Strength! Courage! Give it everything you have, heart and soul . . . . Strength! Courage! Don't be timid; don't get

---

[150] Deuteronomy 34:8, 10-12

discouraged. God, your God, is with you every step you take."[151]

Strength! Courage! This admonition is repeated often in the story of Joshua. Joshua's call was not primarily to organize the people as a society or to call them to God—though these would indeed be part of his work. He was to be the military commander of a great invasion, and he would need much strength and courage to do it. He began, saying: "In three days we go forward across the river!"

Those whose lands were given them already on the Sinai side of the Jordan—the tribes of Reuben, of Gad, and of Joseph's son Manasseh—had promised to fight for their kin until the entire Promised Land was held. To them, Joshua commanded:

> "Your wives, your children, and your livestock can stay here east of the Jordan, the country Moses gave you; but you, tough soldiers all, must cross the River in battle formation, leading your brothers, helping them until God, your God, gives your brothers a place of rest just as he has done for you."[152]

Meanwhile, like any prudent general and like Moses before him, Joshua sent out two spies to explore Jericho and bring back military intelligence. Sheltered by the prostitute Rahab, they found that Jericho's king and all his people were terrified by stories they had heard of the Israelites' battle power in the wilderness. The enemy was in a panic before a shot was fired or, to be more historically accurate, before an arrow was put to bow or a spear was launched.

Joshua moved the people to the Jordan River, the second body of water they were required to cross on their Exodus journey. At the

---

[151] Joshua 1:2-9
[152] Joshua 1:14-15

Red Sea, forty years earlier, the wind had blown all night, and in the wee hours of the morning they could see their way across. They had dry land on which to put their feet. At the Jordan, the waters were flowing full and deep. This time the people of Israel were asked to put the lessons of their Exodus journey to the test. Crossing the Jordan was a sort of a yardstick to measure their growth, but also a terribly practical and necessary step to enable them to move forward. This time they were asked to wade into the waters *before* they parted, to step out *before* they could see their way forward. The Promised Land was not a sort of happily-ever-after ending to their transformative journey. It was a place of opportunity, and it was made possible by and continued to require every lesson they had learned on that journey.

The priests carrying the Chest of the Covenant, sign of God's presence, took up their position before the people at the river's edge. Twelve representatives of the twelve tribes stood by. Joshua commanded:

> "When the soles of the feet of the priests carrying the Chest of God, Master of all the earth, touch the Jordan's water, the flow of water will be stopped—the water coming from upstream will pile up in a heap."

> And that's what happened. The people left their tents to cross the Jordan, led by the priests carrying the Chest of the Covenant. When the priests got to the Jordan and their feet touched the water at the edge (the Jordan overflows its banks throughout the harvest), the flow of water stopped. It piled up in a heap—a long way off—at Adam, which is near Zarethan. The river went dry all the way down to the

Arabah Sea (the Salt Sea), and the people crossed, facing Jericho.[153]

So the priests stood in the middle of the Jordan riverbed as all the people went across. Twelve tribal representatives were commissioned to bring stones from the place where the priests stood, stones to build a memorial to mark the occasion and the miracle that launched their conquest of the land.

> The Reubenites, the Gadites, and the half-tribe of Manasseh had crossed over in battle formation in front of the People of Israel, obedient to Moses' instructions. All told, about forty thousand armed soldiers crossed over before God to the plains of Jericho, ready for battle . . . . The priests carrying God's Chest of the Covenant came up from the middle of the Jordan. As soon as the soles of the priests' feet touched dry land, the Jordan's waters resumed their flow within the banks, just as before.[154]

Remembering and remaining true, strength and courage, stepping out and wading in before the way is fully clear—this is what it means to take the Promised Land. The biblical book of Joshua is about years of battles and land distribution, circumcision and jihad, the establishment of the plans Moses had made with God for the people, but at a deeper level, it is about staying true to lessons learned

---

[153] Joshua 3:13-16. Amos Nur, geophysicist and Stanford University professor, has done interesting research on the contribution of earthquakes to the crossing of the Jordan and the fall of Jericho. He concludes, "The combination, the destruction of Jericho and the stoppage of the Jordan, is so typical of earthquakes in this region that only little doubt can be left as to the reality of such events in Joshua's time." Nur's work offers evidence that ancient stories can contain information of great historical accuracy. These Jordan-crossing and Jericho-falling miracles become less of instrumentality and more of amazing, impossible timing. See, for example, the article, "Believers Score in the Battle Over the Battle of Jericho," *New York Times*, John Noble Wilford, February 22, 1990.

[154] Joshua 4:12-13, 18

and to realities discovered. The wilderness is a necessary period in the journey of transformation: it sets the dye and tempers the steel and fires the clay of the new ways. It brings us to a vulnerable and strong and willing place—and from there to new possibilities, our Promised Lands. You might say that the people of Israel were increasingly better armed to fight the battles ahead. Psychology suggests this is a good description of what we gain as we grow and heal in psychotherapy.

Increasingly Better Armed

For patients, therapists, and clinical researchers alike, psychological change is frustratingly imperfect. It is a becoming and not an arriving. We would prefer a magic bullet, a perfect pill, or a foolproof technique—something that could transport us from our hurt, pain, and existential human struggle to superb well-being, preferably in ten sessions or less! What's hard to describe is the fact that what we earn with all our work and courage in psychotherapy and in the transformative process is simply a ticket to living the ups and downs of ordinary human life with all its challenges: marriages and jobs, parents and children, human minds and mortal bodies. We are like the Israelites who survived the Red Sea and the wilderness to win more years of conquest and settling and just-making-life-happen in the Promised Land.

Freud wrote to a patient about this frustrating fact: "No doubt fate would find it easier than I do to relieve you of your illness. But you will be able to convince yourself that much will be gained if we succeed in transforming your hysterical misery into common unhappiness. With a mental life that has been restored to health you will be better armed against that unhappiness."[155]

---

[155] Sigmund Freud and Josef Breuer, *Studien uber Hysteria* (Vienna, BW, 1, 75-312, 1895d), *Studies on Hysteria,* (SE, 2), p. 305.

Let me give an example. I like the metaphor of ballroom dancing to describe a healthy relationship: two people with coordinated, beautiful, well-practiced steps moving in harmony with each other. You can watch ABC's "Dancing with the Stars" to see the process of growth unfold. Neither partner drags the other around the floor— neither partner hangs all their weight on the other. They may separate for a time, dancing alone but only briefly, to return to their elegant waltz or sexy tango. The judges will lower the scores of those who lift their partner off the floor or dance separately for too long, or for those with little chemistry or concern for each other.

As I described this in a session, my patient was thrilled—she was a ballroom dancer. She said, "Oh! The therapist is like the dance teacher who's expert and gives you the experience of dancing as it should be!"

"Yes," I said, "And then you go out and dance better with your own partner." The dance lessons, the skills we gain and experience we have—like the lessons learned and the new ways forged in the wilderness time—give us our ticket to the real ballroom. They don't guarantee an enchanted evening, or a princess in glass slippers, or winning on reality TV—but they enable us to join in the fun with more skill, freedom, and joy.

In her well-researched and thorough book, *I Can't Get Over It*, psychologist Aphrodite Matsakis discusses the question of healing from trauma. The psychological damage inflicted by trauma is diagnosed as Acute or Post Traumatic Stress Disorder (PTSD). Symptoms continue to be triggered by reminders of the original trauma and may include anxiety, distressing dreams and flashbacks, feelings of detachment or estrangement from others, irritability, and insomnia.

At a recent meeting of trauma experts, the idea was rejected that healing from trauma meant an overall mental state of positive thinking and positive action—as was the idea that healing can be measured by permanent reduction or elimination of PTSD symptoms. Instead, the experts suggested that trauma survivors consider their progress along the following lines (Harvey, 1995):

-Do you panic less at your PTSD symptoms? Are you able to recognize a PTSD symptom more quickly than in the past?

-Are you increasingly able to comfort and soothe yourself in non-destructive ways when you are suffering from a PTSD symptom or from depression?

-Are you increasingly able to cope with or manage your PTSD symptoms and the strong emotions that accompany remembering or being triggered without harming yourself or others?

-Are you growing in self-respect? Are you increasingly willing to take care of yourself physically and emotionally? Do you spend less and less time and energy deceiving people? Are any of the areas of your life becoming increasingly free from the trauma and its effects?

-Are you able to have nondestructive relationships with friends, co-workers, and intimates? Are you increasingly able to speak up in relationships or to otherwise negotiate in relationships so that you can both have the relationship and get your needs met?

-Are you increasingly able to derive some meaning from the trauma, or your life?

Notice that in many of these criteria the word *increasingly* is used, indicating that these standards are not absolute. Progress is measured by growing toward the goals implied in these questions. Reaching such goals may be humanly impossible.[156]

"Increasingly" and "better armed," but not elevated to human perfection, absolute power, or unshadowed bliss. The Exodus journey of Israel demonstrates exactly this. Let's consider for a moment the pivotal difference between the fiasco of the ten spies and the successful crossing of the Jordan forty years later. The central shift in the identity of the Israelites was from a complaining and fearful slave mentality to that "strong and vulnerable and willing place" my client described, from resentful dependency to mature interdependency. At Moses' first scouting of the Promised Land, ten of the twelve spies had not learned those lessons—the people as a whole had not learned those lessons—and so they were not ready to take the Promised Land.

After forty years of wandering, the Israelites had made that deep shift. They waited on the banks of the Jordan. They saw the water of the river flowing deep and strong at the harvest season when it was often in flood. They held their children, herded their livestock, and carried their tents and pots and pans. Gathered ahead were men, battle-ready, facing who knew what might await them on the other side. Some had kissed their wives and children goodbye for who knew how long. Some knew their precious ones followed behind them, vulnerable and anxious. Armed for combat, the men of Israel were waiting with courage to do what they could. Caring for their families and possessions, the women of Israel were waiting with courage to do what they could. Carrying the Chest, the priests of Israel were waiting with courage to do what they could. As for what they could

[156] Aphrodite Matsakis, *I Can't Get Over It: A Handbook for Trauma Survivors*, (Oakland: New Harbingers Publications, Inc., 1996), p. 242.

not control or change, they rested in the knowledge—learned over long years of experience on their Exodus journey—that God would do what only he could. They didn't know what or when or how that might be, but they had the wisdom to know the difference between their part and God's. Open, ask, listen, and answers will come. They had learned a mature interdependency with each other and God. The priests stepped into the water.

And that made all the difference. They had become increasingly better armed to take the land and to live in a new way. That is what it means to take the Promised Land on a journey of transformation. Psychology suggests that we have a chance to go at life differently because we are becoming different. It gives us a chance to change our life trajectory. A small change of trajectory at point A will mean a big change further along at point B, C, or Z. The new ways give us an opportunity to make something different of the ordinary ups and downs of life, the challenges, the stresses.

Let's consider how Liz and Robert are finding their way from Egypt through the wilderness to take their own Promised Land.

An Eggshell Marriage

"Last time, you said you look at life as constantly changing and each change *is* the experience. It's not about the goal. I've been thinking about that a lot. It's not the perfect house or perfect life . . . If you focus on the journey, maybe the rest comes. I see it more now."

Liz said this recently, after nearly four years of our work together— I'm sure it sometimes has felt to her like forty! She came to therapy those years ago because she wanted to make her marriage better. She had said, "I get nit-picky, clamming up and then I snap . . . . I let him have it and he takes it. I've been mean and miserable for so long he gets defensive. I'd like him stronger, someone I could look up to, who could take charge . . . so *I* do it." She was bitter about her husband's small post-doc salary, bitter about her family's constant moving, bitter about his career prospects. I wondered whether she was more interested in the lifestyle or the man. She said she was not interested in sex at all.

Complicating the imbalance of power in the couple and increasing her bitterness exponentially was the financial dependence the couple had on her parents. Beyond their support of the couple through Robert's graduate school while Liz stayed home with their growing family, her parents had also established a trust fund for Liz. As is so often the case with gifts of money and inheritance, what is meant as loving support and protection can become a double-edged sword. Neither Robert nor Liz fully understood the terms of the trust, this third party to their marital union. Both had wildly different feelings about it: Liz was anxious and afraid of losing it while Robert acted in a laissez-faire manner toward it that enraged her. The trust had been operating for years to divide and conquer this couple. The result was hurt and anger on both sides and an imbalance of power in which Liz maintained a financial control that made Robert feel small. She looked down on his ability to provide for his family while she hungered after his care and providing. They were not far from the slave mentality of the ancient Israelites, both felt resentful and yet dependent. This was their Egypt.

Then Robert got a wonderful job—Liz would have said it was a plague! Despite her howls of pain and protest, he took it and took his family across the Red Sea. She followed him, but bitterly, and a profound change occurred in their imbalance of power—not so much a shift toward balance as a flip of polarity. He now sat in the catbird seat and turned from her as she had previously turned from him. Liz said, "I almost feel like he's divorcing himself from me without telling me." Liz found herself in the wilderness.

In a joint session at this point in time, Robert proposed that the couple settle for "an eggshell marriage." They would present a united face to the world, live together, raise their children, but not invest in any real emotional or physical intimacy as a couple. He summed up his view of things very succinctly, "We'll look married on the outside but be roommates on the inside. Liz wants a kind of security and I don't provide it—ergo, I'm not the right person for her, and as a result, she doesn't meet my needs." In a new community, far from her family, Liz found herself profoundly alone.

Many times I thought she might turn tail and run home, something the Israelites often wished to do. Instead, she stayed with Robert and continued with therapy. She wrestled with her bitterness and her disappointed expectations about her lifestyle. She struggled to forgive and be forgiven. She explored her "clamming up" or "turtle-ing" and avoiding—then resenting and criticizing or giving in and blasting—her childhood solution to problems that had become her adult problem. She began to try to express herself in new ways. She was beginning to learn her own lessons of the wilderness, and she did all this with no encouragement or engagement from Robert, who remained adamantly focused on his career and their children—only. From time to time, to test the waters of intimacy, I would ask, "Any love-making?" The answer was always no.

Two years passed in this way. Finally, and excruciatingly slowly, things began to shift. Robert joined us in session—at first for only fifteen or twenty minutes. A third year passed, and finally the couple began to have a date night, something Robert had been unwilling to do before. Yet still they had no emotional or physical intimacy. At this point, Robert said, "I'm keeping Liz at arm's length, which seems reasonable and fair and responsible to me" given the many years of "humiliations," of feeling "embarrassed and ashamed." He said, "I'm not accommodating anymore, and I like it!"

I said, "Bravo! But this eggshell marriage has been created *de facto*. It is inherently unstable—something or someone will ultimately come along and, like Humpty Dumpy, there will be a great fall." I said a marriage with no sex—when there could be sex—was at risk. I spoke of his finding the courage to risk the vulnerability of re-engagement again—and nothing happened.

Then, a few months later came a Jordan-crossing, Jericho-falling moment. Liz told me, "I felt like we broke down a wall!" Robert, for the first time in years, proposed "fooling around" when they went on vacation, but "on his terms." Liz said yes . . . and waited. The vacation flowed smoothly along but . . . no fooling around. She had nearly given up, thinking that now that her parents were visiting, chances of fooling around had become slim to none. Then one night, she was sitting cozily in bed, reading her book . . .

"He said, 'How about it?' I said, 'Okay.' He said, 'What do you want to do?' I said, 'It's on your terms.' He said, 'We could take a shower or something.' And Susan, I'd just had a shower an hour before and was warm and dry and already in bed, and I'd end up with wet hair again! But I said, 'On your terms!' And we took a shower and were intimate, and it was good!"

Liz had found a strong, vulnerable, and willing place in which to meet her husband in a very new way. Instead of turtle-ing, she asked. Instead of holding the reins of power, she opened herself to his terms. Instead of wanting the lifestyle, she chose the man, and, "for the first time in my life, sex isn't a negative thing!"

Furthermore, Liz had discovered that the shift she made had an effect on Robert even though he wouldn't engage with her in making it. "I would have thought *both* people would need to do the work—but I see that when one person makes a shift, it opens up possibilities for the other person to do what they need to do! If one person does what they need to do, it can open things up for everyone else. It's hard. It's baby-steps . . ."

The long, slow years of therapy are giving Liz and Robert the chance to have a real marriage, to love and make love to each other in ordinary human ways, with all the thrills and spills that implies. It isn't about happily-ever-after, as Liz and Robert will tell you, but the trajectory of their lives is changing. All that they have learned on the journey is enabling them to respond to life and love in slightly different ways. "And it was good!"

Liz chose the journey of transformation and discovered something entirely new. As she said, "It's not about the goal. I've been thinking about that a lot. It's not the perfect house or perfect life . . . If you focus on the journey, maybe the rest comes. I see it more now." Liz may not have realized it, but Jesus said something similar: "But strive first for the kingdom of God and his righteousness, and all these things will be given to you as well."[157] Or in the contemporary language of *The Message,* "Steep your life in God-reality, God-initiative, God-provisions. Don't worry about missing out. You'll find all your everyday human concerns will be met." Learn the lessons of the wilderness, risk wading into the Jordan, and you'll find you are increasingly better armed—you're taking the Promised Land.

Sometimes human stories—whether ancient like the biblical Exodus or contemporary like Liz and Robert's—are helpful to illustrate a complex process like transformation, but sometimes the striking imagery of fantasy can bathe old truths in a clarifying new light. Let's turn again to one of my favorite authors, C.S. Lewis, as he offers another vivid picture of the transformative journey.

---

[157] Matthew 6:33, NRSV

Susan Davis, Ph.D.

Eustace's Undragoning

"There was a boy called Eustace Clarence Scrubb, and he almost deserved it."[158] So begins *The Voyage of the Dawntreader,* one of Lewis' Chronicles of the wonderful land of Narnia. Eustace was that particular sort of boy that can only be called a prig. He was an arrogant know-it-all who complained and sulked. He was cowardly and bullying—which of course always go together. He was the cousin of Lucy and Edmund Pevensie, and he was "accidentally" dragged into Narnia with them, all three finding themselves plopped into the blue-green water of the Narnian sea just yards from the painted prow of the Dawntreader. This was quite a shock to Eustace not only because it was cold and wet, but also because he had always mocked the existence of Narnia and because—as it turned out when he was hoisted aboard ship—he was quite prone to seasickness.

As this story goes on, Eustace continued to be dragged along on adventures not at all to his taste. Then one morning, after a horrible twelve-day storm and a week becalmed, the battered Dawntreader limped into the bay of an unknown island. When Eustace discovered that more work was in store to repair and re-supply the ship, he decided to slip away and give himself a much-needed day off. He wandered off, got lost, got panicked, and found himself in an interior valley far from the sea. More terrifyingly, he discovered himself in the company of a dragon . . . one who crept out of his cave—but thankfully only to die.

Taking shelter in the cave, Eustace discovered more surprises—at least to him. Those better educated in fairy tales would have known immediately what they would find in a dragon's lair: a dragon's hoard, but Eustace didn't know and was quite delighted with his newfound riches. He pushed a golden and diamond-encrusted

---

[158] C.S. Lewis, *The Voyage of the Dawntreader,* Book Five of *The Chronicles of Narnia* (New York: Harper Collins, 1952, 1995), p. 1.

bracelet up his arm, and then, exhausted from his exertion and excitement, he soon fell asleep.

When he woke, terror woke with him. It appeared there was another dragon! Worse, it appeared to be following him! Then, worse beyond worse, Eustace discovered that he himself was the terror he feared. "Sleeping on a dragon's hoard with greedy, dragonish thoughts in his heart, he had become a dragon himself."[159] Adding insult to injury, the bracelet that had fit on the arm of the boy cut cruelly into the throbbing leg of the dragon.

Lonely and frightened, he began to realize that the others were not as selfish and stupid as he had told himself they were. He began to see himself more clearly, too, and to long for the help and company of those whose friendship he had scorned. He flew out of the valley and found the Dawntreader's company bivouacked on the beach—frightening everyone there in the process! They soon came to understand that this dragon had been Eustace. The dragon that had been Eustace began to try to be helpful, as he had never done before.

Then one night, he woke in his cave to see a huge lion standing in the valley, moonlight all around it though there was no moon that night. It came close to him. The dragon that had been Eustace found himself very afraid of the lion, but felt he was being asked to follow it and knew he must. Up into the mountains they climbed until they came to a garden. In the middle was a well, as Eustace said later, "like a big, round bath with marble steps going down into it. The water was as clear as anything, and I thought if I could get in there and bathe it would ease the pain in my leg, but the lion told me I must undress first."[160]

---

[159] Ibid. p. 91.
[160] Ibid. p. 107.

Eustace was confused by this command since, as a dragon, he wasn't wearing any clothes. Then he thought, snakes shed their skins—perhaps this was what the lion meant. He scratched and scratched, and soon his whole scaly, knobby skin came peeling off, but beneath he found another skin just like it, and when that one was torn and scratched off, another. Eustace described what happened next:

> "Then the lion said—but I don't know if it spoke—'You will have to let me undress you.' I was afraid of his claws, I can tell you, but I was pretty nearly desperate now. So I just lay flat down on my back to let him do it.
>
> "The very first tear he made was so deep that I thought it had gone right into my heart. And when he began pulling the skin off, it hurt worse than anything I've ever felt . . . . And there was I as smooth and soft as a peeled switch and smaller than I had been. Then he caught hold of me—I didn't like that much for I was very tender underneath now that I'd no skin on—and threw me into the water. It smarted like anything but only for a moment."[161]

Splashing in that night-dark pool, Eustace found himself a boy again, restored to himself. He had gotten himself dragoned, the outward manifestation of his inward state, his Egypt. He crossed the Red Sea when he sought the others on the beach that day. His wandering in the wilderness had consisted of his dawning awareness of reality, the reality of who he and others had actually been and of the problem he now constituted for them. Following the lion—the Great Lion Aslan, son of the Emperor-over-the-Sea, though he did not know it—and allowing himself to be "undressed" by him, Eustace stepped into his Jordan. Lewis' beautiful metaphor of the scratching off of Eustace's dragon skins suggests that band-aid fixes

---

[161] Ibid. p. 108-109.

will really not suffice. We've got to go for the whole, deep, painful, heart-changing, life-transforming process.

Here is how Lewis ends the adventures of Eustace and describes taking the Promised Land:

> It would be nice, and fairly nearly true, to say that "from that time forth Eustace was a different boy." To be strictly accurate, he began to be a different boy. He had relapses. There were still many days when he could be very tiresome. But most of those I shall not notice. The cure had begun.[162]

Taking the Promised Land—increasingly better armed—we broke down a wall—he began to be a different boy: all these phrases capture a sense of the ongoing nature of the transformative journey. Eustace's story and the Israelites' can be considered parallel at several points. Like the dragon that had been Eustace in his lonely cave, the Israelites began to be a different people as they wandered in the wilderness. As he followed the lion that frightened him, they waded into the Jordan while it was still flowing deep with no clear way across. They had each come to a vulnerable, strong, and willing place. Each found transformation and new life, their Promised Lands, though there were still many times when they forgot their wilderness lessons and turned back to the old ways. But something had changed, a shift, "it's a mystery how it happened."

Like Eustace and the Israelites, Liz and Robert found a vulnerable, strong, and willing place from which to cross the Jordan. "I felt like we broke down a wall!" That small beginning can change the trajectory of the whole story by the end. To be strictly accurate, we might say Liz and Robert began to be a different couple. They have relapses. There are still many days when they can be quite distant

---

[162] Ibid. p. 112.

and hidden from each other, but most of those we will not notice. The cure has begun.

They talked over his exodus,
the one Jesus was about to complete in Jerusalem.
Luke

Chapter Nine:
Scapegoating, Surrender, and Seeds

One of the fascinating and marvelous aspects of ancient Hebrew poetry is that it depends on structural parallelism, not rhyme scheme, for its artistry. The poet states each idea in pairs of images and in parallel phrases. Consider this example: "They surrounded me like bees; they blazed like a fire of thorns."[163] Or this, in which the first two and the last elements are comprised of parallel couplets:

> Where can I go from your spirit?
>> Or where can I flee from your presence?
> If I ascend to heaven, you are there;
>> if I make my bed in Sheol, you are there.
> If I take the wings of the morning
>> and settle at the farthest limits of the sea,
> even there your hand shall lead me,
>> and your right hand shall hold me fast.[164]

---

[163] Psalm 118:12, NRSV
[164] Psalm 139:7-10, NRSV

Not only does this convention make it easy to appreciate the poetry of the phrasing in any language into which it may be translated, but it enriches our understanding of the poetry since each member of the pair illuminates the meaning of the other.

The story of the Exodus of the ancient Israelites and the story of Jesus of Nazareth can be seen in the same way: as yoked and parallel metaphors, each member of the pair illuminating the meaning of the other. These two powerful stories stand at the center of two of the world's great religions, each story very different on the surface but each fundamentally concerned with the same deep truth of transformation. The Exodus story has not only deepened my work as a psychotherapist, it has given a new dimension to my understanding of the beloved Jew from Galilee, Jesus, descendent of the Israelites who took the Promised Land. His teaching, death, and resurrection stand against the backdrop of that story and its map of the transformative journey. The Red Sea, the wilderness, the Promised Land—Gethsemane, the tomb, a risen rabbi—these images direct our attention to the same revolutionary, life-changing process of transformation.

The writer of the New Testament letter to the Hebrews was very clear in linking the stories of the Exodus and of Jesus of Nazareth together. He detailed the history of Israel we have been examining: from Abraham to Joseph, Moses to Joshua and beyond. Then he wrote: "Therefore, since we are surrounded by so great a cloud of witnesses, let us also lay aside every weight and the sin that clings so closely, and let us run with perseverance the race that is set before us, looking to Jesus the pioneer and perfecter of our faith . . ."[165]

I like to imagine the ancient stadium in Olympia, filled with those who have already run their races, cheering as they watch us compete in our turn. Bright banners, smell of sweat and olive, hot sun on cool

---

[165] Hebrews 12:1-2, NRSV

stone, the sound of tears and cheers, shouts of encouragement and advice! Some in the stands are those whose names we know: Abraham and Sarah, Joseph and his brothers, Moses and Zipporah, Joshua and Caleb. Some are those who shared their experience of the race in creative expression: Gerard, Henry, Jack, Sheldon, Joseph, Langston, Robert. Some of those in the stands are from the generations that came before: for me, Lillian and Archer and Bob. I imagine some of those whose lives we've watched in these pages sitting in the front row, mopping the sweat from their brows as they take a break from their own heats, watching and cheering as we run ours.

Jesus is there under the King's canopy, wearing his crown of thorn and laurel, his gold medals gleaming in the sunshine, cheering and coaching. How did he run the race? How does he coach us on running the same race? Let's explore what we can learn about the process of transformation from him.

Jesus' Exodus

I tremble as I begin to write this section. To discuss Jesus' exodus story—the Gethsemane choice, crucifixion and tomb, and resurrection—is a weighty task, especially in a book written by a psychologist and focusing not on the spiritual but on the psychological journey of transformation. Yet the psychological and spiritual overlap in the depths of our psyches and the stages on Jesus' road through Jerusalem parallel the stages of the Exodus journey of his people to the Promised Land. In fact, in Peterson's description of Jesus' transfiguring, mystical experience on the mountain, he makes the parallel explicit:

> While [Jesus] was in prayer, the appearance of his face changed and his clothes became blinding white. At once two men were there talking with him. They turned out to

be Moses and Elijah—and what a glorious appearance they made! They talked over his exodus, the one Jesus was about to complete in Jerusalem.[166]

We'll discuss only those aspects of Christ's passion that may illuminate our understanding of the transformative process, leaving aside questions of theology or divinity. Instead, we'll focus on the ways that psychology brings depth and gives perspective to Jesus' journey through the garden of Gethsemane to the garden that held the tomb.

Egypt: The Human Condition

Jesus' journey, as ours, begins with the security/slavery of our human condition. Bounded by time and space, subject to physical and social and familial limitations, Jesus was a human being like we are. He lived in Israel during the time when Pontius Pilate was governor, about 30 CE. In about 90 CE, the historian Josephus wrote:

> At this time there appeared Jesus, a wise man. For he was a doer of startling deeds, a teacher of people who received the truth with pleasure. And he gained a following both among many Jews and among many of Greek origin. And when Pilate, because of an accusation made by the leading men among us, condemned him to the cross, those who had loved him previously did not cease to do so. And up until this very day, the tribe of Christians (named after him) has not died out.[167]

Living in a particular time and place, with a particular family, language, and culture, in a particular physical body, Jesus was truly

---

[166] Luke 9:29-31
[167] Josephus, *Jewish Antiquities*, book 18, as reconstructed and translated by Meier in *A Marginal Jew*, vol. 1, p. 61, and quoted by Marcus Borg, *Jesus*, p. 30.

"of Nazareth," his hometown. He ate and drank and slept and sweated and wept and laughed. Though for him the spiritual world was a present and every day reality, he also walked along the shores of the Sea of Galilee surrounded by the physical world and within the human experience we all share.

Perhaps the ultimate Egypt is our human condition as material and physical beings—what Paul called "the disordered mess of struggling humanity."[168] It is an existential reality that is familiar but painfully limited, one within which we are not intended merely to stay. It is here that Jesus' life, ministry, and transformative journey began.

The Red Sea: Gethsemane

It is clear from the Gospel accounts that Jesus knew the risks of embarking on and continuing his ministry of preaching, teaching, and healing. He knew that the reaction of the religious and political establishment was uneasy at best and enraged at worst—and he continued to confront them directly and indirectly, by word and deed, throughout his ministry. Marcus Borg paints his portrait as a "religious revolutionary."[169] Since the Jewish temple hierarchy held both political and religious power, his continued course was dangerous and unlikely to end well, from a human point of view.

Yet he stayed the course. He continued to draw more followers, continued to confront the religious authorities, all of this threatening and angering them more and more. Events began to escalate and Jesus intentionally intensified them. Choosing the Passover celebration—perhaps intentionally linking his transformative journey with the Exodus of his people—he made a triumphal entry into Jerusalem amidst cheering crowds. Then he celebrated the Passover meal—now

---

[168] Romans 8:3

[169] See the full title of Marcus Borg's book, *Jesus: Uncovering the Life, Teachings, and Relevance of a Religious Revolutionary.*

ritualized in the Christian Eucharist or Communion—with his disciples. He continued to recognize and predict where all this was likely to lead him: "this is my body . . . this is my blood, God's new covenant . . . I'll not be drinking wine again until the new day when I drink it in the kingdom of God."[170]

Then Jesus went out to a garden called Gethsemane, outside the city walls of Jerusalem. He went to pray and to face his own Red Sea decision. Although he clearly knew the path he had been on, just as the Israelites knew the risk they took in leaving Egypt, this was the final moment of truth: the irrevocable choice to go forward.

> He plunged into a sinkhole of dreadful agony. He told [his disciples], "I feel bad enough right now to die. Stay here and keep vigil with me."

> Going a little ahead, he fell to the ground and prayed for a way out: "Papa, Father, you can—can't you?—get me out of this. Take this cup away from me. But please, not what I want—what do *you* want?"[171]

Thy will be done. Jesus' Red Sea choice to go forward was made sweating blood in Gethsemane, but please, not what I want—what do *you* want? Apparently a free will choice is an absolutely agonizing and necessary part of the transformative journey. Burning bushes, plagues, and even religious authorities may prod us toward it, but in the end we must choose what we will do with what is happening to us. "Tell the people to go forward!" God told Moses. The old ways or the new—bitterness or mercy and grace, patience and love, truth and justice—my will or thy will be done.

---

[170] Mark 14:22-25
[171] Mark 14:33-36

The Wilderness: the Crucifixion and the Tomb

Events played out quickly after that choice was made. Jesus was deserted by his frightened followers, examined by the religious authorities who attempted to trip him up with perjured witnesses, scourged and mocked by the Roman soldiers under Pontius Pilate who went against his own better judgment for the sake of political expediency. Jesus was killed on a cross, reviled and attacked by the very crowds who had earlier followed him seeking miracles.

This last point is one worth exploring and one we will return to later in this chapter. The crowds who had shouted, "Hosanna!" were replaced by those screaming, "Crucify him!" The crowds who had eaten their fill of miraculous loaves and fishes, sitting in thousands on the grass above the Sea of Galilee, were replaced by those hungering for his humiliation and death. The longed-for Messiah had become a scapegoat. "People passing along the road jeered, shaking their heads in mock lament: 'You bragged that you could tear down the Temple and then rebuild it in three days—so show us your stuff! Save yourself! If you're really God's Son, come down from that cross!'"[172] What a shocking reversal.

Jesus endured this physical and emotional pain inflicted by human beings. Then, in his final moments, he experienced that deepest of existential terrors, the sense that the Universe is empty. That God is not there. He cried, "My God, my God why have you abandoned me?"[173] Alone, in pain, abandoned, afraid, Jesus was like the children of Israel in the wilderness who felt lost when Moses did not come down from the mountain, but unlike them, he clung to his faith and to his hope. In his cry of abandonment, he was quoting Psalm 22:1, written by David ten centuries before. The psalm prophetically captures Jesus' pain and the pathos—and our

---

[172] Mark 15:29-30
[173] Mark 15:34

own wilderness experience—but ends in praise and an affirmation
of future blessing.

> My God, my God, why have you forsaken me?
> Why are you so far from helping me,
>> from the words of my groaning?
> O my God, I cry by day, but you do not answer:
>> and by night, but find no rest.
> . . . . I am a worm, and not human;
>> scorned by others, and despised by the people.
> All who see me mock at me;
>> they make mouths at me, they shake their heads;
> "Commit your cause to the Lord; let him deliver—
>> let him rescue the one in whom he delights!"
> . . . . I am poured out like water;
>> and all my bones are out of joint;
> my heart is melted like wax;
>> it is melted within my breast;
> . . . . you lay me in the dust of death.
> . . . . They divide my clothes among themselves,
>> and for my clothing they cast lots.
>
> But you, O Lord, do not be far away!
> O my help, come quickly to my aid!
> I will tell of your name to my brothers and sisters;
> In the midst of the congregation I will praise you:
> All the ends of the earth shall remember
>> and turn to the Lord;
> and all the families of the nations
>> shall worship before him.
> . . . . And I shall live for him.[174]

---

[174] Psalm 22, NRSV; excerpted verses

Then Jesus, "with a loud cry, gave his last breath."[175]

Still Jesus' wilderness ordeal was not finished. Joseph of Arimathea laid Jesus' body in his own tomb and sealed it with a stone. Since it was the eve of the Sabbath, Jesus was left in the tomb from Friday evening to Sunday morning. It was a time of darkness and death. Some of the early creeds say, "He descended into hell."[176] Those who loved him were in grief and despair and deep hopelessness, lost and wandering.

Taking the Promised Land: the Resurrection

On Sunday morning, some of the women who had followed Jesus went early to the tomb with spices to embalm him.

> They worried out loud to each other, "Who will roll back the stone from the tomb for us?" Then they looked up, saw that it had been rolled back—it was a huge stone—and walked right in. They saw a young man sitting on the right side, dressed all in white. They were completely taken aback, astonished.

> He said, "Don't be afraid. I know you're looking for Jesus the Nazarene, the One they nailed on the cross. He's been raised up; he's here no longer. You can see for yourselves that the place is empty. Now—on your way. Tell his disciples and Peter that he is going on ahead of you to Galilee. You'll see him there, exactly as he said."[177]

---

[175] Mark 15:37

[176] The Apostle's Creed, developed by the church in the first two centuries after Jesus' death as an affirmation of faith, is still used by western Christian churches, both Catholic and Protestant.

[177] Mark 16:1-7

And so it was. Jesus appeared and spoke to many people.[178] Sometimes he appeared in a closed room, sometimes on the road, sometimes at the lakeshore. He showed his wounded hands, feet, and side. He ate fish. He was not a ghost, yet he appeared and disappeared in ways no human could. People didn't recognize him—then suddenly they did. It was Jesus transformed, someone familiar and beloved yet substantively brand-new; something very rich and very strange.

Later, Paul tried to explain the resurrection transformation:

> Some skeptic is sure to ask, "Show me how resurrection works. Give me a diagram; draw me a picture. What does this 'resurrection body' look like?" If you look at this question closely, you realize how absurd it is. There are no diagrams for this kind of thing. We do have a parallel experience in gardening. You plant a "dead" seed; soon there is a flourishing plant. There is no visual likeness between seed and plant. You could never guess what a tomato would look like by looking at a tomato seed. What we plant in the soil and what grows out of it doesn't look anything alike. The dead body that we bury in the ground and the resurrection body that comes from it will be dramatically different.[179]

The metaphor of seeds is one Jesus also used—it is clear from his teaching that he was not a sort of unconscious, accidental hero on the cross. He knew exactly where the journey of transformation, his exodus, was headed all along. Earlier, he had said, "Listen carefully: unless a grain of wheat is buried in the ground, dead to the world, it is never any more than a grain of wheat. But if it is buried, it sprouts and reproduces itself many times over. In the same way, anyone who holds onto life just as it is destroys that life. But if you let it go,

---

[178] Beyond the Gospel accounts, see Acts 1:3 and I Corinthians 15:3-8.
[179] I Corinthians 15:35-38, 42-44

reckless in your love, you'll have it forever, real and eternal."[180] In every gospel, he made this message explicit, perhaps most succinctly in Luke: "'Those who try to make their life secure will lose it, but those who lose their life will keep it.'"[181] Here Jesus is speaking to the frightening paradox he pioneered for us, that, as in the well-known prayer attributed to St. Francis, "It is by giving that we receive, it is by pardoning that we are pardoned, and it is by dying that we are born to eternal life."

These are hard truths. A seed must be buried and "dead to the world" to grow, and bloom, and bear fruit. We must give up the old to discover the new. We must leave Egypt to find the Promised Land. Jesus' stories suggest that if we cling to Egypt, the known and familiar and secure, in the end we will lose even that. But if we risk leaving the security that has become slavery—as Peterson's *Message* puts it, "reckless in our love"—for the hero's adventure of transformation, of becoming whole, we will find our lives and life itself. It requires a leap of faith, the road less traveled. As my client said, it's a mystery how it all happens. Resurrection. Transformation.

Let's turn from this mystery—the something brand new represented by the resurrection and arrived at via Gethsemane, the cross, and the tomb—to psychological ideas that may shed more light on the inner workings of the transformative process for us.

Polarized Positions and Projective Identification

One universal of human experience is to have been someone little in the care of someone BIG. As a babe in someone's arms, we are dependent, vulnerable, needy, and very little. The one who holds us is independent, powerful, self-sufficient—in our eyes, anyway—and

---

[180] John 12:24-25
[181] Luke 17:33, NRSV

very BIG. Now, as humans we are always both little *and* BIG, dependent *and* independent, vulnerable *and* powerful, needy *and* self-sufficient. Remember that the transformation for the Israelites in the wilderness was from a whiney and manipulative neediness to an interdependency with God and each other—what my client called a "strong and vulnerable and willing place." In other words, the Israelites had to move from feeling little to doing what they could—from wanting to be BIG to trusting where they were needy. They had to become little *and* BIG, vulnerable and powerful, an integration of both. This is the substance of the Serenity Prayer and the natural outcome of human growth and maturation.

What happens if it's not okay to be both little and BIG? What happens if our caretaker needed us to be little—or needed us to be BIG? A mild form of this occurs commonly with oldest and youngest children: the oldest whose mother may have needed her to be BIG, the youngest whose mother may have wanted him to stay little. A more extreme and destructive form occurs in abuse: the abusive parent/bully is BIG while the vulnerable child/victim is little. These situations make it hard to create an integration of little and BIG.

When we cannot integrate, we split off what is unacceptable and bad and repress it. That is what Jung means by the Shadow, but what is repressed is not inert. When we repress the Shadow, it finally leaks, explodes, or implodes. One way this occurs is projection. We project that which we cannot face within ourselves onto others, seeing it as theirs and not ours, casting them as actors in our own unconscious dramas. We take polarized and polarizing positions, being BIG to someone else's little or vulnerable to someone else's power.

Melanie Klein, working in the mid-1900s with disturbed children, came face to face with some very dramatic, primitive, and polarized stuff: love and hate, reparation and destructive envy, generosity and greed. She witnessed what happens when we humans are unable to balance and integrate our inner darkness and light, and instead unconsciously split within ourselves and repress what we cannot face. She saw polarizing and projection taking place in children's dreams, fantasies, and relationships. She also saw that projection doesn't work very well unless the person on whom we project identifies with the projection, carries it for us, and so enters into our improvisational psychodramas with us. But if they do—reacting in anger to our projected power, or as a victim to our projected vulnerability, or as hero to our projected gold—a powerful system begins to be formed. She called this two-step reciprocal process, "projective identification."

We can go further. The one identifying with our initial projection can initiate a complimentary projection with which *we* identify in turn. A perfect feedback loop is formed. People become locked into relationships of mutual projective identification, all unconsciously— an experience that may sound odd but that is common in all of our lives. Who is that person you cannot stand? Who is that person who, as Johnson said, begins to glow for you? Projective identification.[182]

An everyday sort of example may help illustrate. A man has had a bad day, arriving home feeling disrespected and enraged. As he walks in the door, he may unconsciously project his anger onto his wife, expecting her to be angry. He reacts to this assumption, behaving all unaware in ways that elicit actual anger within her. Perhaps he makes a zinger of a comment under his breath or a joke whose cruelty can be denied, or perhaps he ignores everyone, retreating behind his computer screen—again. She completes the feedback loop by becoming irritable and bitchy; she identifies with his projection. Suddenly he doesn't feel angry anymore. Instead, he feels self-righteous and ill-used in a martyred sort of way. Meanwhile

---

[182] For an extended discussion of this concept, see Thomas H. Ogden, "On Projective Identification," *The International Journal of Psycho-Analysis,* (1979) 30, 357.

she and the kids wonder what happened. She was perfectly cheery before he came home. In this way, he relates to the rejected aspect of himself in her, seeing it as hers, while keeping it separate from his conscious sense of himself. This is a compromised sort of solution for him, but it leaves everyone unhappy.

Projective identification plays out at the level of groups and nations as well. We project the Axis of Evil onto terrorists as they project the Great Satan onto us—mutual projective identifications of BIG and little, bully and victim. In this way we split bad from good and hatred from love, avoiding awareness that we are both good and bad, little and BIG, and so are they. While this happens between groups, it can also happen within a group. As in all defensive processes, this one is triggered by anxiety, stress, threat, and disruption. The group suddenly turns against one of its members, blaming, attacking, and ultimately rejecting and even ejecting him or her from itself. We call this process "scapegoating."

Scapegoating has a long history. The word itself comes from an old biblical translation of the ritual for purification and atonement that Moses instituted in the wilderness. A living goat was chosen by lot, the high priest laid his hands on its head and confessed all the sins of the people, then led it out of the camp. "The goat will carry all their iniquities to an empty wasteland; the man will let him loose out there in the wilderness."[183] Hence "[e]scape goat," the goat who escaped. Unfortunately for the goat, and really making the phrase an oxymoron, Levitical tradition evolved to ensure that the goat did not make its way back to human habitation. They pushed it off a cliff.

Examples of scapegoating abound: from the courtroom to the boardroom, from the playground to the highest echelons of academia, from the playing field to the battlefield. After World War I, a humiliated and impoverished Germany found in their Jews a perfect

---

[183] Leviticus 16:22

scapegoat. Even the language of their propaganda is that of the projection of the Shadow: non-Aryan pollution threatening their racial purity, dark threatening light. CEOs, college presidents, and heads of state—or perhaps their second-in-commands—find their heads on the chopping block when their companies, universities, or countries are stressed and in crisis.

René Girard, renowned French anthropological philosopher, brought attention to the power and importance of the scapegoating mechanism.[184] Focusing on literature, history, and anthropology, he traced scapegoating throughout history and particularly in the development of archaic religion, sacred ritual, myth, and taboo. Though Girard did not attribute the underlying mechanism of scapegoating to projective identification, I think that Klein's idea offers great explanatory power to his observations.

Girard saw that social groups respond to crisis and destabilizing stress by finding a scapegoat, often someone who is from the outside, or marginalized in some way, or guilty of some crime. Sometimes it is a leader who is above and therefore not quite of the group. The people turn from fighting each other to attacking the scapegoat, joined and united by this common antipathy. They are projecting their fear and vulnerability onto the scapegoat, impassioned in their attack and destruction of it. When the scapegoat or "victim" identifies with the projection, he or she completes the projective identification with feelings of guilt, fear, bitterness, or shame. Then the scapegoat does indeed carry the sin and darkness of the people into the wasteland. In the aftermath, order, peace, unity, and goodness are restored in the group, at least for a time. Girard said that in this way, violence becomes sanctified and ritualized in religious ceremony so that it is played out again and again in hopes of maintaining the calm that descended after the murderous storm. Threat and stress, projection

---

[184] René Girard, *The Scapegoat* (Johns Hopkins University Press, reprint edition), 1989.

and blame, attack and scapegoating are followed by a temporary restoration of order and peace.

Girard concluded that the crucifixion of Jesus was an enactment of the sacrifice of the scapegoat. "But it is a sacrifice that refutes the whole principle of violence and sacrifice. God is revealed as the 'arch-scapegoat,' the completely innocent one who dies in order to give life. And his way of giving life is to overthrow the religion of scapegoating and sacrifice . . ."[185] Let's consider the crucifixion in the light of scapegoating and projective identification.

Scapegoating and Projective Identification: the Crucifixion

When we consider projective identification as the psychological mechanism for scapegoating, it begins to be clear how Jesus' death was the result of this unconscious process and how it transformed the polarized split of scapegoating into something altogether new. In his crucifixion, the crowds and priestly aristocracy and Roman imperial powers split and projected their personal and collective Shadows onto the figure hanging on the cross. It was a perfect storm of projection: "You bragged that you could tear down the Temple and then rebuild it in three days—so show us your stuff! Save yourself! If you're really God's Son, come down from that cross!"[186] What is this but saying, "Jesus, you thought you were BIG, doing miracles and saying you knew God! But you are little and *we* are BIG! You are weak and *we* are strong!"

It was a world where Roman imperial power bullied Jewish religious aristocracy that in turn bullied the ordinary human peasant. BIG and little, bully and victim, were passed along in a chain of falling

---

[185] René Girard as quoted in an interview by Brian McDonald, "Violence and the Lamb Slain," *Touchstone*, December 2003, http://www.touchstonemag.com/archives/print.php?id=16-10-040-i.
[186] Mark 15:29-30

dominoes. Finally, the crowds had an opportunity to project all their littleness, their victimhood, their dependency and impotence. All Jesus needed to do was to accept everyone's projection, to be the scapegoat victim who carried away the hated and rejected parts of everyone else![187] Jesus' death has many facets and layers of meaning. The ideas of projective identification and scapegoating illuminate one: that Jesus' death was demanded by the frightened and frightening splits within our collective human psyche.

Jesus, however, did not accept and identify with these projections of the victim. When Pilate, for example, suggested that Jesus should be more forthcoming, considering that Pilate held his life in his hand, Jesus said, "You haven't a shred of authority over me except what has been given you from heaven."[188] Jesus did not identify with the projections onto him as a scapegoat, and so he truly transformed the entire process and taught us how to do the same. His behavior as he hung dying exemplified the principles he himself had taught for healing and integrating these splits—teaching we will explore more explicitly in a few pages.

Healing the Split: The Tomb as Wilderness

The place of healing the split, taking back the Shadow, and integrating polarities is "uncomfortable and un-stabilizing." It is the experience of the wilderness. It is scary, anxiety provoking, and unpredictable. We have given up the old, but the new has not yet come. We are like the hermit crab naked, vulnerable, and exposed on the beach.

---

[187] Note that this was also the basis of the first two of Jesus' three temptations as he started his ministry. In Matthew 4:3-6, Satan begins by saying, "If you are the son of God..." Jesus must have wondered at the audacity of his call, the *BIGness* of it in the context of the world's view of his littleness as a landless peasant carpenter. The taunt and his temptation then, "If you are so *BIG*, prove it! Show it! See! You are *little!*"

[188] John 19:11; See also Jesus' discussing this power to lay down or take up his life in John 10:17-18.

"He descended into hell," as the old creeds say. Whatever else that means, it conjures the experience of the wilderness.

The tomb is a perfect image for this phase in the transformative process. Dark, silent, still, in between. Nothing seems to be happening, as when a caterpillar lies within its cocoon. The Scriptures are silent. It is as though the universe is holding its breath. Yet the caterpillar is becoming a beautiful winged creature within its chrysalis, and Jesus would be resurrected from within the tomb, the scapegoat become the Lamb of God. It's a mystery how it all happens.

The tomb communicates one aspect of the transformation process. Wandering in the wilderness communicates another. From the outside nothing seems to be happening. On the inside, as we have seen, changes are occurring as lessons are learned, identity is changed, new ways are discovered and practiced. Piaget's adaptation process is occurring as we revise our conceptions of ourselves and of the world. It is the wilderness and the tomb, and all of it leads to something very new—taking the Promised Land. Resurrection.

Wholeness and Transformation: the Resurrection

The resurrection teaches us about the something rich and strange, familiar yet new, of the transformative process. In resurrection, the old is brought forward, transformed, as a caterpillar to a butterfly, a seed to a tomato plant, Jesus of Nazareth to Jesus Christ. Jesus was still Jesus. In the beautiful story concluding the gospel of John, Mary Magdalene lingered near the tomb in grief and confusion. When she turned, she saw a man she thought was the gardener standing there. It was not until he spoke her name that she recognized him.[189] He was something new, yet Jesus nonetheless.

---

[189] John 20:11-17

This is the sort of something brand new that comes as a result of the transformative process we are exploring. This is what we mean by the Promised Land. This is what happens when that which has been polarized is no longer projected. Instead, the Shadow is integrated with the self, creating a new wholeness. We'll explore that wholeness further in the next chapter. For now, let's simply say that the Shadow and the self are both changed as they encounter each other—"now that fiend and I are such good friends the other's each." What would it look like to be both little and BIG? What would happen if the bully and the victim merged? What would it mean to be strong *and* weak, independent *and* dependent? Can you imagine it?

To help us imagine, let's see what it looks like as Brooke and Matthew work to break projective identifications and integrate polarities. Remember that Brooke described herself as the maiden in need of rescue and Matthew as her knight in shining armor—a perfect feedback loop of mutual projective identifications. Yet during her transformative process, Brooke began to take back her gold and to discover her inner hero. As she did so, she broke a feedback loop, freeing Matthew to wrestle with his own Exodus journey.

Crisis on the Board

Matthew began our session: "Insomnia still. It cycles, but I've had it for so many years now." He was concerned that he wouldn't be at the top of his game for the board of directors meeting he would be attending the next week on the east coast. With the time change, his insomnia, and the concerns he had over resolving a problem that had developed with a couple of members on one of the subcommittees, there was a lot to keep him awake at night.

We began to explore the insomnia, the symptom, as a part of himself that he hated and rejected, his Shadow side and perhaps a burning bush. I asked what his insomnia could be saying to him or doing for him—since all parts of the Self are acting in the service of the Self. He said, "It's like self-sabotage. It's like it's saying to me, 'Stop *doing* all the time!' I like to be in control of myself, disciplined. I think I'm afraid that if I don't keep *doing* I won't be as good—I'll be just okay, average. When I wake up in the night, if something is on my mind, that's okay. I'll figure out what to do about it, but if nothing is on my mind but just anxiety, I won't go back to sleep!"

Matthew hated his insomnia but, worse than that, he hated the idea of slowing down, of not "doing," of not performing at the top of his game. He adhered to a disciplined daily schedule, sometimes ribbing or outright criticizing Brooke for sleeping in—even on vacation—or allowing their young son to eat anything but the healthiest of food. Every day he exercised, he meditated, he listened to self-help tapes, he worked, he arrived home for a glass of wine with Brooke, had dinner. Then he went to bed, woke up, and couldn't sleep. That frustrating insomnia! After his concerns about Brooke's moods, it was really the only fly in the ointment.

Early in our work together, I found myself mentally preparing to bring *my* A-game to our sessions: a sort of emotional limbering up after my high carb breakfast, putting on my mental track shoes. With Matthew, I felt like I was running next to a speeding train, trying to keep up and not wanting to disappoint. I liked him a lot. He was invariably warm and considerate toward me, but the opening lines of the "Adventures of Superman"[190] came to mind:

> Faster than a speeding bullet! More powerful than a locomotive! Able to leap tall buildings at a single bound! ("Look! Up in the sky!" "It's a bird!" "It's a plane!" "It's

---

[190] Based on the comic books first published in 1938 by Jerry Siegel and Joe Shuster and sponsored by Kellogg's, the original television series began airing in 1952.

Superman!") Yes, it's Superman . . . strange visitor from another planet who came to Earth with powers and abilities far beyond those of mortal men! Superman, who can change the course of mighty rivers, bend steel in his bare hands, and who, disguised as Clark Kent, mild-mannered reporter for a great metropolitan newspaper, fights a never-ending battle for truth, justice, and the American way!

When I shared this feeling of racing to keep up, Matthew laughed and admitted that he had heard that feedback before. Brooke complained that he wanted to "fly above it all" and "not get stuck in the details." His executive team commented on "my people skills . . . maybe I'm a little aloof—I'm always moving." He acknowledged that, though they liked him, people didn't feel connected to him and maybe even felt insecure.

Matthew had learned not to slow down, except as insisted upon by his frustrating insomnia. What was he running from? The answer lay in my feelings of trying to keep up with him and in his admission that people felt disconnected from him and insecure around him. We might say that Matthew's insomnia was trying to alert him to a BIG/little split within his own psyche. His effort to stay BIG while repressing and projecting little could be felt by others: for example, in my need to bring my A-game and even in Brooke's feelings of shame and inadequacy. Superman was trying to escape his inner Clarke Kent.

This interchange shifted our therapy interactions—I felt I could leave my mental track shoes home from then on. But though Matthew could see some value—on the margin—of slowing down to let people connect, his moving, doing, and performing had been tremendously successful both personally and professionally. Why change it?

Childhood Solutions and Adult Problems

Matthew was the youngest child and only son of a powerful, utterly self-focused, financially successful father and a charmingly social but anxious mother. The children were molded by Dad's authoritarian and sometimes abusive rule and by Mom's refusal to acknowledge any negative feelings and her admonition to show up, be positive, and go along. He'd learned early what advantage it was to be "the good boy," the teacher's pet, the scholar-athlete, the golden boy, and the family mediator. He'd learned to smile and go along, to work hard and achieve. This was very effective in getting what he wanted—his parents and siblings adored him, he got straight A's, his father was proud and didn't interfere—but if it wasn't, he could still go for what he wanted—as his mother did—indirectly.

As an adult, his ways of coping continued to be very effective. He had blazed his own successful, lucrative, and rapid career path—tending to move on quickly after only a few years in any given job. By forty, he'd made his first ten million. Even if new ventures didn't prove as successful, he wasn't too disturbed. He kept performing and going along and disciplining himself to dismiss, as his mother had, any negative or vulnerable feelings that might emerge. Finally, he found himself poised to take over the top spot, becoming CEO of a wonderful, progressive, creative company. After some painful politics with the previous CEO who had been part of the founder's executive team, Matthew's "dream job" became a reality.

Meanwhile, the previous CEO moved onto the board amongst a group of old cronies. Matthew had invited several members to join the board as well, so it consisted of an old and new guard. With his energy and charm, his gift for bringing in money and making it grow, the board was initially happy with their new CEO. He was fast, friendly, and focused—but fighting with his wife and sleeping fitfully at night.

Part of his childhood solution involved splitting off any aspect of himself that didn't fit the good boy, the golden boy, the positive boy who went along. Any complaint, any weakness, any desire to dawdle or to dabble, any sense of inadequacy had no place in his world—and besides, he cared about and took care of his loved ones. He learned early to be disciplined and busy to compensate for any weakness and to avoid feeling helpless or little. If that didn't work, projection did. He could feel strong and independent while caring for someone who felt weak and inadequate. This caretaking was not consciously manipulative—he *was* a good boy and he *did* care.

When he met Brooke, she was passionate, creative, and beautiful—but also divorced, depressed, and with young dependents. They fell madly in love and were married. The rescuing hero and the battered and bruised maiden rode off into the sunset, a perfect storm of projective identification piling up at the horizon. Unhappy as he was—on the margin—with Brooke's unhappiness, he was very happy with his happiness.

Yet he couldn't sleep. That storm cloud refused to dissipate. So that's where we started in therapy that day. I continued to press him: "So what would happen if you were just okay, just average?"

He said, "I wouldn't feel good about myself."

I asked, "And what would happen if you didn't feel good about yourself?"

"I don't like power exerted over me," he said. "If I'm not great, there's no room to negotiate . . . Like with my Dad. There was never room to negotiate with him. He had all the power."

Matthew had grown up with the polarities of little and BIG, and he had come up with a solution: become BIG so no one could make you feel little. By running and doing, by performing and impressing,

Matthew avoided anyone exerting power over him. He could fly high over the heads of the competition. He was praised and admired and allowed to do what he liked, and he *liked* to do what he liked and had found a way to ensure that he could: by becoming Superman, the rescuing hero. This strategy also ensured that if, for some reason, someone didn't like what he did, he could very successfully ask forgiveness—but could usually avoid the humiliating experience of asking for permission.

Recently those gathering storm clouds were beginning to produce thunder and lightening—less in his marriage at the moment, as Brooke held her ground against their pattern of mutual projective identifications—but on the board. The fact that there was an old and new guard—and the presence of the former CEO whose resentment about being usurped by Matthew could not be bought off with financial success—created unstable atmospheric conditions. Then, like a Washington politician, Matthew tried to usher something through a subcommittee, hidden in the fine print. It wasn't that there was anything unethical or wrong with what he wanted to do, but he didn't want to ask permission, to feel little. He didn't want anyone to have power over him.

The chair of the subcommittee, someone who had been competitive with Matthew from the start, was enraged. Thunder rumbled. Storm clouds darkened and spread. Another member on the committee, one of the new guard whom Matthew had always counted on for support and approval, called him angrily to berate him for his below-board strategy. The board chair held him out of the first round of meetings. The board began to move into a scapegoating mode, splitting and projecting their own Shadows of greed and power and egotism onto Matthew. He was not greedy, bullying, or egotistic, but his style—rapid moving, independent, indirect-if-necessary—made him seem arrogant and out for himself. Not trusting them, he had acted in a way that made them feel they couldn't trust him. Afraid of being little, he had made others feel little and move to get their power back. No wonder he couldn't sleep.

I now knew what Matthew would have to do in order to stem the storm of scapegoating and projective identification on the board, what he would have to do to become increasingly better armed and more whole. He would need to surrender—to the appropriate authority of the board and to awareness of that small boy within himself with all his feelings of vulnerability and insecurity. If he appeared to his board as a lone ranger, a maverick out for himself, could he be powerful enough to surrender to their mandate and their role? If he'd rather ask forgiveness, could he instead choose to ask permission? Could he slow down and focus on his relationships with the board members? Not alliances and triangles, not backroom coalitions and deals, he needed to go direct and one-to-one, to consult, to ask, to acknowledge. This was the opposite of everything he usually did, and the opposite of the behaviors that were triggering the board's projections. To stem the scapegoating tide and calm the rumbling storm, he must be powerful enough to feel vulnerable.

What would Matthew look like if his rescuing hero and his damsel married and merged? What would it look like if he were both Superman and Clark Kent simultaneously, if they were integrated into one super but human man? As we began simply to ask these questions, Matthew was on the threshold of reversing the polarization and projection he was experiencing with his board. He didn't like it and it certainly didn't feel safe, baring his throat to the wolves. It felt a lot more like being hung on a cross or maybe just out to dry, but it was the most powerful and efficient way to disconfirm the projections, to break himself and his board out of a process of mutual projective identifications. It was the most powerful and efficient way to stop the scapegoating that had begun and would inevitably continue unless a fundamental shift was made in who he was—not merely on the margin of what he did. More, it would integrate the polarities that kept him from his inner wholeness and his Promised Land.

Jesus' Coaching

Sometimes I tell these stories of the Exodus, Jesus, and patients like Brooke and Matthew to my clients. They always ask me, "Okay, so how do you do it? How do you stop projecting and identifying with projections? How do you become both BIG and little?" Psychology says we must become aware. We must meet the total stranger knocking living the hell out of us so that we might make new choices and become something new, something rich and strange. Jesus taught us that though this feels like death, it is the only way to new life. Furthermore, he gave some very practical if revolutionary coaching about how to go about it.

Jesus said, in effect:

> don't project—
> don't identify with others' projections, only God can show you who you are—
> don't act out on the projections of others, instead transform them. Here's how . . . .

Don't Project

Jesus hated hypocrisy wherever he found it, and he found a lot of it among religious people, thus steering straight into the rage of the religious establishment of his time. He confronted this hypocrisy— this split and repression, or polarization within the self—over and over again. Jesus warned again and again against judging, blaming, criticizing—the result of that split and polarization. In other words, he said that projecting our own dark, little, lusting, or bullying impulses onto others and then attacking and condemning them is hypocritical and not the way of God's kingdom. It is not the new way better aligned with reality and with what is most Real, his loving Father. "Why do you see the speck in your neighbor's eye, but do not notice the log in your own eye?"[191] As we understand projective identification, Jesus might be saying: don't project—take responsibility for your own Shadow—integrate the BIG and little, love and hate, good and bad within yourself—open yourself to the transforming power of God. Don't project!

Don't Identify

He also taught that we do not need to identify with the projections of others. For Jesus, God's love for us is the only source of our identity, our true selves. "What's the price of a pet canary? Some loose change, right? And God cares what happens to it even more than you do. He pays even greater attention to you, down to the last detail—even numbering the hairs on your head! So don't be intimidated by all this bully talk. You're worth more than a million canaries."[192]

Peter Marshall, Presbyterian pastor and chaplain to the Senate in the late 1940s, was a man for whom God was a living presence. In his sermon, "Praying is Dangerous Business," he said:

> It is a wonderful idea, once it gets hold of you, that God loves you,
>   whoever you are . . . for yourself.
> You are precious to Him.
>   He loves *you*.
>   He wants you to be happy.
>   He wants to give you good things.
> It is His will for you that life should be full,
>   abundant . . .

---

[191] Matthew 7:3, NRSV
[192] Matthew 10:28

and rich.

He expects us to believe that he holds us in the hollow of His hand,
    And that we are safe for all eternity.

This does not mean that no trouble shall come to us—[but that]
    God will not permit any troubles to come upon us,
        unless He has a specific plan by which great blessing
            can come out of the difficulty.[193]

"It is a wonderful idea, once it gets hold of you," that your only identity is as loved and chosen by God. If we know who we are as God's beloved children, that we can go nowhere away from his Spirit and that darkness isn't dark to him, then we are able to recognize and integrate our own Shadows. If we have begun to recognize and integrate our own Shadows, we will be less overwhelmed and more able to withstand the Shadow projections that will inevitably, no matter how lovely or loving we are, come our way.

Transform Projections with Love

"There is a great irony here: proclaiming so much love, experiencing so much hate! But don't quit. Don't cave in. It is all well worth it in the end. Don't be bullied into silence by the threats of bullies. There's nothing they can do to your soul, your core being. Save your fear for God, who holds your entire life—body and soul—in his hands."[194]

Jesus was very clear about the fact that projections will occur and pull us to respond, but he is very practical about how to avoid acting on the projections sent our way. I've always noticed that the God's

---

[193] Catherine Marshall, *A Man Called Peter: The Story of Peter Marshall* (Grand Rapids, Michigan: Chosen Books, a division of Baker Book House Co, 1951, 2002), p. 357.
[194] Matthew 10:22, 28

advice is very practical—difficult to choose to do sometimes, but very simple and down-to-earth.

> "Here's another old saying that deserves a second look: 'Eye for eye, tooth for tooth.' Is that going to get us anywhere? Here's what I propose: 'Don't hit back at all.' If someone strikes you, stand there and take it. If someone drags you into court and sues for the shirt off your back, gift wrap your best coat and make a present of it. And if someone takes unfair advantage of you, use the occasion to practice the servant life. No more tit-for-tat stuff. Live generously.

You're familiar with the old written law, 'Love your friend,' and its unwritten companion, 'Hate your enemy.' I'm challenging that. I'm telling you to love your enemies."[195]

In other words, Jesus is saying that when someone acts BIG because they feel little, when they fear your BIGness even when you don't know you are BIG, when they suddenly turn the psychological tables on you and you find yourself feeling incredibly small—don't try to be BIG and don't believe you are little. When someone projects their fear onto you by hating you, don't fear them and hate them back—love them! "No more tit-for-tat stuff. Live generously." Then Jesus got even more down-to-earth and practical and told us exactly how to do it.

Pray and Forgive

Love. That's a big word. How do we break the projective identification feedback loop by loving those who are projecting onto us? The first recommendation Jesus had was that we can pray for them. Jesus taught, "Love your enemies and pray for those who persecute you."[196]

---

[195] Matthew 5:38-44
[196] Matthew 5:44, NRSV

Or, in Eugene Peterson's words, "When someone gives you a hard time, respond with the energies of prayer, for then you are working out of your true selves, your God-created selves."[197] When we pray for those who are projecting on us, we will be surprised at how much easier it becomes not to identify with their projections—for now we are working out of our true selves, and then we might be surprised by what happens to them.

In my senior year in high school one of the guys on my cheerleading squad—I'll call him George—seemed to be making it his personal mission to make my life a living hell. I couldn't make a mistake without his mocking laughter, couldn't say a word without seeing him turn to a friend to gossip. Since our squad practiced every day after school, this was a lot to take. Then, worse, he attended my Young Life club, adding Monday nights and weekend retreats to his venues for tormenting me. One club talk, our leader suggested that we pray for our enemies. I thought, "That would be George!" I sure didn't feel love, but I began to pray for him every day.

A few weeks before graduation, I saw George coming toward me in the hall between classes. I thought, *Oh, no! What now?* To this day, I remember myself standing stunned as George said he had given his life to God at last weekend's retreat—and then asked me to forgive him for his treatment of me. I realized that for all this time, George had been wrestling within himself over this decision. His discomfort and fear about changing his life battled with his longing for God and a more abundant life—and it all played out as he mocked, shamed, and belittled me. He was trying to avoid dying to his old self, leaving Egypt and crossing his own Red Sea. Praying for your enemies might not involve a dramatic conversion experience . . . but it might!

The Prayer for your Enemies is a powerful way to practice Jesus' recommendation to love as well as a powerful way to keep our

---

[197] Matthew 5:44

identities grounded in God's reality, his love and mercy. I like the phrasing of the yogic meditation of loving kindness:

"May [my enemy], be well—
   may he [or she] be filled with peace—
      may he [or she] feel love."

The Prayer for your Enemies is unselfish. We do not pray that our enemies will see the error of their ways—much as we would like this to happen! We must pray that prayer for ourselves as David did.[198] We pray simply for their individual blessing today. Alcoholics Anonymous suggests doing this for fourteen days. This prayer works outside of time and space and without a direct word or action—whether our enemies are living or dead. It has huge transformative power, not only for ourselves as we avoid identifying with projections, but also for situations, for others, and sometimes even for our enemies themselves. Loving our enemies by praying for them is very transformative.

Then Jesus took this loving of enemies further in a second practical but revolutionary and very, very difficult recommendation. He said, "Forgive." The process of forgiveness—and it is a process begun simply by an act of the will—sometimes by choosing to be willing to *become* willing to forgive—may take a lifetime to complete. I like a definition I heard once that forgiveness is the decision to let go of our demand that the past should be different. It is certainly not denying that the past was what it was. It is certainly not suggesting that we should recreate that past again in the present. Forgiveness is not even as helpful, necessarily, for our enemies as it is for ourselves. It is another way to step away from the projections and identifications that keep us stuck.

---

[198] See Psalm 139:23-24

Forgiveness is extolled in every one of the world's religions, but psychology has rarely given enough focus to this ancient and wise recommendation for avoiding the splits and feeling of being stuck created by projective identifications. [199] Jesus was uncompromising about the necessity to forgive,[200] and, of course, on the cross he practiced what he preached: "Father, forgive them; they don't know what they're doing."[201]

If anger, hatred, intimidation, destructive envy, weakness, smallness, or inadequacy is being projected on us by behaviors that effectively elicit those experiences in us, we can only break into the feedback loop by recognizing what is happening and then neither identifying with nor behaving in ways that confirm those projections. Otherwise we create a self-sustaining feedback loop, a closed system that goes round and round without changing anything. The bully continues to bully and hide from his inner vulnerability—the victim continues to be the scapegoat and hide from his inner power. The split in each is never healed. Only by breaking into the feedback loop, by taking back our own projections and by refusing to identify with the projections of others is the system destabilized and the polarization integrated.

A colleague in graduate school spoke of this process this way: "You've got to hunker down like a rock; neither withdraw nor attack." This is exactly what Jesus taught and what he himself did from Gethsemane to the cross: he neither withdrew nor attacked, neither projected nor identified with projections. This is what René Girard said Jesus did to overthrow the religion of scapegoating and sacrifice. Blamed and condemned, he knew who he was—victimized, he chose to give

---

[199] Note the excellent work of Frederic Luskin, PhD., of the Stanford Forgiveness Projects. His research with those who have lost loved ones to violence in Northern Ireland has shown decreased rates of depression, anger, and stress, and increased optimism and hope. See his website: www.learningtoforgive.com.
[200] Matthew 18:21-22
[201] Luke 23:34

his life—hated, he loved by praying for his enemies and forgiving them.

That's what the crowds are cheering and what Jesus is coaching as we run our race. That's the way that the death and resurrection of Jesus parallels the Exodus journey of transformation: the Red Sea and Gethsemane, the wilderness and the crucifixion and the tomb, the Promised Land and Easter morning. This is what moves us toward the wholeness that is the purpose and end of the transformative journey. Polarities and projective identifications broken and integrated, surrender embraced as strength, dying for resurrection life—"I'm about to do something brand new. It's bursting out. Don't you see it?"[202]

---

[202] Isaiah 43:19

Weeping may linger for the night,
but joy comes with the morning.
David

"Don't stop. Further up and further in! Take it in your stride."
Jewel the Unicorn

Chapter Ten:
Further Up and Further In!

At the end of *The Last Battle*, Lewis' Narnian Chronicle about the end times of Narnia and the first experience of Aslan's country, the joyous cry is "Further up and further in!" The miracle is that the further up and further in they went, the further and faster they could go. In fact, in Aslan's country, as Tumnus the Faun explained, "The further up and the further in you go, the bigger everything gets. The inside is larger than the outside."[203]

It is the same with the transformative journey, once you begin. Psychological growth is like a spiral going further up and further in. We find ourselves in familiar territory again and again, but each time we understand a little better, choose to go forward a little sooner, implement our new ways a little more easily, and find ourselves a little more whole. Increasingly better armed, in a strong

---

[203] C.S. Lewis, *The Last Battle*, (New York, HarperCollins Publishers, 1958, 1994), p. 207.

and vulnerable and willing place, we are more and more able to keep our eyes on the goal. We have begun to be different people and the cure has begun.

Deeply Human, Fully Alive

Throughout this book, I've used stories from Scripture and Lewis' fantasy literature to illustrate the transformative process and the something rich and strange that results from it, but I don't want to leave you with the impression that there is anything fairy tale or even miraculous about it. In fact, transformation is a process that is natural, organic, and very much a part of our human experience. Its action in our lives makes us much more deeply human, much more fully alive.

A couple of years ago, a beloved professor of mine visited. R. Fenton Duvall was ninety-two years old, and professor emeritus of history from Whitworth College in Spokane, Washington. I hadn't seen or spoken with him since I transferred schools after my sophomore year until a reunion brought us back into contact and a trip to California brought him to my door. One afternoon we drove over the Golden Gate Bridge to Sausalito and a favorite restaurant overlooking the city and the bay. I took pictures along the way and later that evening loaded them onto my computer.

As I examined the photographs, I came across one from the restaurant. "Oh, no," I groaned, "I don't think you're going to like this one!" I had caught Dr. Duvall, head thrown back in joyous laughter, his few strands of silver hair awry, mouth wide open and teeth a little scraggily and straggly. It wasn't flattering—did I mention he was ninety-two? Dr. Duvall turned the laptop to look at the screen. "Well, that's the way I look, isn't it?" he said with warmth and humor. Such humanity and humility! Such self-acceptance, genuineness, and freedom. Dr. Duvall had come to such wholeness through his lifelong walk with God. Sainthood is the result of wholeness, as Robert Johnson said, and wholeness is the result of the transformative journey. That sainthood, that wholeness, is what St. Irenaeus meant when he said that the glory of God is a human being fully alive.

Natural and Organic

At the same time that transformation is natural, organic, and human, it is neither magical nor mechanical. We can facilitate it, but we cannot make it happen. We can create the right conditions for it, but we cannot force it anymore than we can pull a tulip out of its bulb or a walnut tree out of its nut. The thrust for life, the mechanism of growth, and the DNA pattern for the mature plant are already contained within the seed. In its time and on its own, life, growth, and maturity will manifest. The plant can be crippled, or stunted, or destroyed, but it cannot be manufactured. Even today with cloning techniques, we can only copy what Nature creates in infinite variety, mixing and matching in a test tube but then allowing the inherent, natural process of growth to occur on its own.

Metaphors of nature, plant-life, and gardens come easily when we discuss this natural and inherent thrust for growth and wholeness—in other words, the transformative energy—within each of us. Jesus said it's "like seed thrown on a field by a man who then goes to bed and forgets about it. The seed sprouts and grows—he has no idea how it happens. The earth does it all without his help."[204] We can choose and we can intend, but it's a mystery how it all happens, as my client said. The transformative process is not something we can initiate, hurry, or even avoid by purposely willing it. It can begin with burning bushes or with plagues, with dreams and symptoms,

---

[204] Mark 4:26-27

or with tragic events and scary opportunities. It can begin within or without.

Jung wrote:

> When I examined the course of development in patients who quietly, as if unconsciously outgrew [their former] selves, I saw that their fates had something in common. The new thing came to them from obscure possibilities, either outside or inside themselves; they accepted it and grew with its help.
>
> But the new thing never came exclusively from within or without. If it came from outside, it became a profound inner experience; if it came from inside, it became an outer happening. In no case was it conjured into existence intentionally or by conscious willing, but rather seemed to be borne along on the stream of time.[205]

At the Red Sea, we saw that transformation requires a choice to go forward. In the wilderness, we saw that it requires opening ourselves to the new ways and the answers that come but may not be what we expect. Yet, even when we choose to open ourselves to transformation, we cannot make it happen—we cannot conjure it "into existence intentionally or by conscious willing"—and we don't have to. The process is a natural one, and the potential for it lies within each one of us. It is the result of something deep within our psyches reaching for wholeness. It is the result of something deep within us crying, "further up and further in!" It is the result of the Holy Spirit working in the depths of who we are, so that we "simply embrace what the Spirit is doing in us."[206]

---

[205] Carl Jung, *The Wisdom of Jung*, ed. Edward Hoffman (New York: Kensington Publishing Corp., 2003), p. 48.
[206] Romans 8:4

Susan Davis, Ph.D.

Acorn to Oak: Psychological Views

Psychologists and psychoanalysts have used different terms to describe this natural developmental and transformative process. Psychologist Abraham Maslow, best known for his hierarchy of human needs, and humanistic psychologist Carl Rogers called it self-actualization. Jung called it individuation. Karen Horney, early neo-Freudian psychoanalyst, called it self-realization. Irvin Yalom discusses the impact Horney's ideas had on his own developing thought and career:

> When I was finding my way as a young psychotherapy student, the most useful book I read was Karen Horney's *Neurosis and Human Growth.* And the single most useful concept in the book was the notion that the human being has an inbuilt propensity toward self-realization. If obstacles are removed, Horney believed, the individual will develop into a mature, fully realized adult, just as an acorn will develop into an oak tree.

> 'Just as an acorn develops into an oak . . .' What a wonderfully liberating and clarifying image! It forever changed my approach to psychotherapy by offering me a new vision of my work: My task was to remove obstacles blocking my patient's path. I did not have to do the entire job; I did not have to inspirit the patient with the desire to grow, with curiosity, will, zest for life, caring, loyalty, or any of the myriad of characteristics that make us fully human. No, what I had to do was to identify and remove obstacles. The rest would follow automatically, fueled by the self-actualizing forces within the patient.[207]

---

[207] Irvin D. Yalom, *The Gift of Therapy,* (New York: Harper Collins Publishers, 2002), p.1.

"Just as an acorn develops into an oak." Just as a plant, stuck in too small a pot in the corner of a dim office, will green, thrive, and grow when transplanted, fertilized, and given enough water and light. Just as a spring clogged with garbage and debris—a rusting old truck, leaking cans of toxic paint, rotting bananas—will flow cold and clear when all that debris is removed. Just as a clan living in a security that had become slavery, like the Israelites in Egypt, becomes a new and thriving nation when they journey through the wilderness and risk the Promised Land. Just like that, when we remove obstacles—childhood solutions to problems, fears and old coping strategies, perceptions and meanings and identities that don't fit—we become something brand new, something rich and strange, It's a mystery how it happens.

At least a few times a week, my patients ask perfectly beautiful and flabbergasting questions. How do I play? Find courage? Become creative? Know what I feel? Know what I want? I don't have to answer those questions, which is a good thing because I don't know the answers to those questions. Those qualities and capabilities are part of our inherent humanity. Therefore they are capabilities we all have—unless they are blocked or obstructed in some way. The journey of transformation, the Exodus journey, is the process of removing obstacles so that the potential life and self within each of us may begin to grow naturally. The security that has become slavery is the state of being blocked by those obstacles. Burning bushes and plagues force us to confront them. The Red Sea choice to go forward is a choice to go past them. The wilderness is a time of discovering what life could be like beyond those obstacles as we develop a new identity and learn lessons about surviving and thriving in the world.

The wilderness lessons for the children of Israel had to do with giving up the old ways of a complaining and manipulative dependence, a slave mentality. Their lessons had to do with growing into the new ways of a balanced interdependency in which they had the courage and strength to take the responsibility they could while trusting God and each other for the help they still needed. That interdependency is the integration of polarities—autonomy and connection, independence and dependence, strength and weakness, courage and vulnerability. It is about becoming whole. The integration of polarities, the process of becoming whole and balanced, flexible and resilient, fully ourselves and fully alive, is the purpose of the transformative journey. In those powerful yoked and parallel metaphors, the stories of the Exodus and Jesus, it is the Promised Land and it is the resurrection life.

The Wounded Healer

So, no, I don't want to leave you with the impression that the transformative journey is magical or miraculous—it is deeply and inherently natural and human. And I don't want to leave you with the impression that the Promised Land, this wholeness, this something rich and strange we've been discussing, is a fixed point that we achieve once and for all in our mortal lives. The transformative journey is neither "once upon a time" nor is it "happily ever after."

Last week a patient and I were discussing her frustration in not feeling as connected to God as she once had. I suggested that feelings tend to ebb and flow, that part of maturing in faith, as in any love relationship, involves holding on through the darkness, the wilderness times in our lives. She cried out, "But it's been five years!" I heard her anguish and confusion. How do we maintain faith and hope during these painful and often frustratingly prolonged periods in our lives? I said, "Yes, and still it's true." Then she said, "But, Susan, why doesn't anyone in church ever talk about it?"

Her pain, her loneliness, her confusion have stayed with me. I resonate with her feelings only too well. I am writing a book about the transformative journey and I believe it with every fiber of my being, but let's talk about it. I, too, know those long dark years when I had made the choices to grow, to heal, to choose wholeness and God, and yet . . .

I remember one evening the week before I completed my predoctoral year and left Hawaii. I was sitting alone in the cooling sand on a beach in Waikiki as the setting sun flamed the sky red, orange, and purple. It was my Red Sea choice point: would I move ahead with my transformative journey even as I returned to California and the life I had there—whatever the cost, and I knew it would cost—or would I go back to my old life and my old ways of being in the world? I was worried about the cost, some of which I suspected and some I had not yet realized. I thought of Jesus' words, "Seek first his kingdom and his righteousness, and all these things shall be yours as well."[208] Later that night I wrote in my journal: "'His kingdom'—Lord, for me to seek your kingdom is to be a healer. 'His righteousness'—somehow this seems to be about becoming the whole self I was created to be. Lord, I give you my heart. And body and mind and soul. Let your will be done! And while it is being done—hold me in your love." Not what I want, but what you want.

When I sat on that beach in Waikiki in the fading glow of those flaming colors, with all my heart I know that I chose his kingdom and his righteousness. Yet I did not leap into the Promised Land, nor was the killer whale dream the last of its kind. Over the next couple of years, I continued to have frightening dreams of whales and dolphins. Then one night I dreamt *I was riding a black horse bareback, his flanks wet with sweat. His name was Prince.* When I woke I thought, "Wet, black skin . . . the killer whale has morphed into a land animal. And I'm riding him!" Somehow I'd made a step forward in my relationship with my Shadow and a step forward in

---

[208] Matthew 6:33, RSV

my view of it as something helpful and perhaps even noble, princely. Months later, in another dream, *I came upon a black man lying in a puddle in the middle of a road in the middle of the night. I brought him home and put him in my bed.* Wet, black skin but now a man—a man I brought home to my bed! Another step forward, yet still I could not say toward what.

Though I did not fully understand my dreams' imagery, it was clearly about something I identified as masculine, something I associated with power and with the body, the sensual and physical world. Raised in my Christian home with my charming, athletic, powerful father, I longed for his attention and love but grew to fear it, too. I was afraid of his criticisms of me like the nipping of tiny tropical fish, the anger fueling his booming preacher's voice, the undercurrent of sexual darkness he carried that I did not recognize nor understand for many years. So while I longed for love and intimate connection, I learned to fear excess of passion in all its forms: sexuality and sensuality, anger and assertiveness, intensity and intimacy, conflict and competition. I learned caretaking and achievement as a compromise between that longing and those fears, a compromise that became a bind and a prison for me as I split off my own power and passion. I'm pretty sure I got in the way of the power and passion of those I loved, too. My task was to embrace this very passion and power, my Shadow, as well as my own vulnerability and need. My task, like that of the children of Israel, was to find the interdependency of doing what I could while trusting others and God to do what only they could.

As these dreams played out, marking a slow transformative process within, life in the external world continued in its challenging way. Feelings ebbed and flowed, opportunities opened and closed, people came and went while I held on and God held me. Last month I had another dream, the first in many years that I could identify as of killer whale lineage. The imagery had morphed again, this time from fear into attraction and from killer whale into the professional ballroom dancer known as the Bad Boy of the Ballroom, Maksim Chmerkovskiy. (I do enjoy ABC's "Dancing with the Stars!") Maks is an athlete and a fierce competitor. He is often caught on film fighting with his partners and sometimes with the judges, but I notice that he fights with his partners for their full participation and finest performance, for the excellence of the dance, their enterprise together. When they "leave it all on the floor," as they say on the show, he can be surprisingly protective and tender.

At first I thought this dream held nothing new, just the same frustrations, longings, and fears I have always known in finding an intimate connection with a man. Then I began to think . . . perhaps Maks is actually me. Perhaps I need to embrace and be embraced by my inner Maks. In my imagination, he is like my killer whale and like my dad: powerful and passionate and therefore dangerous, intense and capable of fighting ferociously, but perhaps also of loving fiercely. If he is within me—if within me lies all that power, passion, ferocity, and love—then I can safely surrender to trust in another because I trust in myself. I can be strong and vulnerable, but not in a compromised caretaking sort of way. I can come from a strong, vulnerable, and willing place within myself. Increasingly better armed, I can be a wounded healer who is herself becoming healthy and increasingly more whole. Further up and further in!

Racing News and Updates

Let's check in on a few of the races being run by others we've met in these pages. Writing and publishing a book is its own transformative journey, and transformative journeys take time. You may have read the last few chapters in the last few days or weeks, but for my clients and for me, the living of it has taken the last few years.

In that time, Sarah's husband has further embraced his addiction to alcohol and almost completely withdrawn from every loved one. Her children are growing beautifully despite the heartbreaking experience of, as her youngest wrote, their dad choosing alcohol over them. Sarah herself is emerging a deeper and wiser woman and is beginning to turn her face beyond the emptying of her nest to the new life, the Promised Land ahead for her.

Pete has struggled hard the last few years, holding onto his business in tough economic times, but he has resolved his difficult divorce, entered into a meaningful new relationship, and begun to trust and believe in himself.

Cindy and Josh have ended their engagement, but both are continuing to discover their paths to wholeness. Josh is in graduate school and following his sense of call to work with inner city youth. Cindy is learning to draw clear boundaries between herself and her parents as she comes to understand the realities of their characters. Difficult as this is, she is being challenged to choose to live her life as she believes she must, neither fully and foolishly trusting nor hopeless in the face of human darkness as it plays out within and all around her. Not that this is always true. There are still plenty of times when she is discouraged and hopeless, but the cure has begun.

I had not seen Sylvie for a few years when she called and came in last week. Although she wanted to talk about her difficult marriage, she also wanted to report on great successes. She has gotten her degree and a great job, and has almost completed her supervised hours for licensure. Her kids are flourishing, but even more importantly, "I don't say I'm a terrible therapist anymore—I'm not beating myself up! When my dad died five years ago, I felt like I'd lost my cheerleader, but somehow I started to do it for myself. It has been so hard for so long, but I've grown so much. I'm feeling super, super, super blessed."

Bernadette's boys are sprouting like bean stalks. She says, "I have a lot of challenges, but now they don't defeat me or define me. That voice is *in me*. The old doormat? Been there, done that!"

Liz and Robert are still working to come together in an intimate marital relationship as they raise their kids and build their lives together. Robert has begun to stand up for himself—first for his kids and his role as father, and now for his marriage and his role as husband. "I will not be emasculated!" is his mantra. As he does, Liz on her part is called to be present, to ask, suggest, and respond instead of hiding, stewing, and then snapping. Who knows what will happen next?

Matthew is still exploring how to integrate his power and his vulnerability, and to own his own negative feelings in his relationship with Brooke. He is discovering a new capacity for leadership in his business and in his family. As he has begun to exert that presence and leadership, his relationship with Brooke is deepening in a way that is thrilling to them both.

Just last week Brooke experienced one of those beautiful moments of joy and awareness of her own growth that come on the journey. She said:

> "My life took off ahead of me and forgot to inform me! It's surreal. Layne the Bane of My Existence, the one who turned everyone on the church committee against me, wanted to meet with me. She said, 'I know I need to make things right with you. Will you forgive me?' There is something going on in my life, and I am overwhelmed by it!
>
> And then, you know how I wanted to be on a board so badly, to have a stake, a say in something I cared about? I'm on two boards now, both serving underprivileged kids, and

if I chose a board I'd want to serve with, I couldn't make this up!"

She continued thinking through what has happened for her in this transformative journey:

"The difference between me now and me then is that now I'd go directly to a person and say, 'Can we talk?' I'm strong enough to listen to their criticisms and reflect, because I'm not afraid to own my own power. I don't understand what happened; there's been such a shift without me being on the front line of intention. I see that all I needed to do was put my stake in the ground and be pure in my intention, but to take one step at a time.

It's so funny. It's the classic hero story. The hero is reviled and bullied by others, is the outcast and is misunderstood, but he learns to take on all the slings and arrows and still know who he is while being open to test and question himself. Maybe you need to check yourself and adjust, but you keep going. And the hero prevails, and all those people who vilified him are cheering, even though he is not trying to win anyone over."

The transformative journey is about ordinary human beings finding a path, in very simple but very new ways, often with setbacks and unexpected challenges, to life and wholeness. "And the hero prevails."

The Ghost and the Red Lizard

There is one more race for us to see before we close. In chapter five, I promised I would tell you the end of the story of the Ghost and the Red Lizard from *The Great Divorce*. I think of this imaginative story as a sort of time-lapse film of the transformative journey mapped in the Exodus. Let's look at the last few moments of the race as the Ghost passes over the finish line and enters the Promised Land, that resurrection wholeness Jesus showed us is possible.

Remember that, enslaved to a compulsion and an addiction; the Ghost was caught in his very familiar Egypt, his personal hell. You may remember the struggle the Ghost had in allowing the Angel to kill the Lizard who sat whispering on his shoulder. His burning hand close to the Lizard, but waiting for the Ghost's free choice to go forward, the Angel asked again and again, "May I kill it?" Finally, in great agony, the Ghost cried out his assent, and in that moment crossed his own Red Sea. The Angel took, broke, and threw the Lizard to the ground.

In amazement, the Narrator watched as a great transformation took place in both the Ghost and the Lizard. This is the wilderness journey at warp speed. The Ghost grew solider and, bit by bit, became a huge and golden man. The Lizard writhed and grew until "what stood before me was the greatest stallion I have ever seen, silvery white but with mane and tail of gold. It was smooth and shining, rippled with swells of flesh and muscle, whinnying and stamping with its hoofs. At each stamp the land shook and the trees dindled."[209] Then Lewis paints a beautiful portrait of what we have been calling the Promised Land, resurrection life, and wholeness. I'll continue the story in Lewis' own text, impossible for me to improve upon.

> The new-made man turned and clapped the new horse's neck. It nosed his bright body. Horse and master breathed each into the other's nostrils. The man turned from it, flung himself at the feet of the Burning One, and embraced them. When he rose I thought his face shone with tears, but it may have been only the liquid love and brightness (one

---

[209] C. S. Lewis, *The Great Divorce*, (New York: Simon & Schuster, 1996), p. 100.

cannot distinguish them in that country) which flowed
from him. I had not long to think about it. In joyous haste
the young man leaped upon the horse's back. Turning in
his seat he waved a farewell, then nudged the stallion with
his heels . . . . Already they were only like a shooting star
far off on the green plain, and soon among the foothills of
the mountains . . . .

While I still watched, I noticed that the whole plain and
forest were shaking with a sound which in our world would
be too large to hear, but there I could take it with joy . . . .
It was the voice of that earth, those woods and those
waters. A strange archaic, inorganic noise, that came from
all directions at once. The Nature or Arch-nature of that
land rejoiced to have been once more ridden, and therefore
consummated, in the person of the horse.[210]

The Narrator and his mentor discuss this stunning picture of
transformation. "What is a Lizard compared with a stallion? Lust
is a poor, weak, whimpering, whispering thing compared with the
richness and energy of desire which will arise when lust has been
killed."[211] Like resurrection, the transformative process does not
ultimately destroy or leave behind anything of worth. What is best
is finally brought forward to a new fulfillment and wholeness. What
must be let go is finally restored to its rightful place and balance.
This is not rebirth, starting over again at the very beginning, *tabula
rasa*, wiped clean but essentially of the same nature. Instead, it
is resurrection as we are transformed into right relationship with
ourselves and others, God and the Creation itself, recognizable yet
new. The Lizard becomes a stallion rightly related to and serving
his master. Lust becomes passion and desire rightly integrated into

---

[210] Ibid. p. 100-101.
[211] Ibid. p. 102.

the whole nature of the man, and restored human nature takes its rightful place in relationship to the whole of Nature.

Joy Comes with the Morning

If wholeness is the result of transformation, joy is our experience of that growing wholeness. The journey of transformation is not easy, as we have seen. It is the hero's journey, an Olympic athlete's race, marked by blood, sweat, and tears, but those who are on the journey and running the race say that it is all worth it. In describing his own experience of that transformative journey, Paul said, "I'm not saying that I have this all together, that I have it made. But I am well on my way . . . . I'm off and running, and I'm not turning back!"[212] David said, "Weeping may linger for the night, but joy comes with the morning," or, as Eugene Peterson put it, "The nights of crying your eyes out give way to days of laughter."[213]

Joy in the morning and days of laughter come because the experience of a growing wholeness, that something rich and strange we are developing into, is liberating and wonderful. A client of mine has been becoming increasingly more aware of his split-off and repressed Shadow power. The merged symbol of a "bunny-dog"—his unconscious comment on his conscious identity—had turned into a tiger in yesterday's dream: *I cried out in warning, "You can't open the door! The tiger will get out!"* As he has begun to meet his inner power in his dreams—and though he is still afraid of it—in his waking life he has found himself surprised at how free and glad he is feeling, even in the midst of some difficult personal circumstances. He said, "You know, I think the source of my joy is this sense of *potential*."

---

[212] Philippians 3:12, 14
[213] Psalm 30:5, NRSV and *The Message*

The misery and grief of Egypt and the anxiety of the wilderness became the longed for Promised Land, flowing with milk and honey, abundant with grapes and figs and pomegranates. The dark nights of Gethsemane, the crucifixion, and the tomb, gave way to the joy and laughter of Easter morning and resurrection life. Crabbed and compromised lives and selves give way to the joy of "this sense of potential."

On the wall of my office, I have a framed photograph. It's me, floating in the turquoise waters of Cozumel, grinning from ear to ear, holding a dolphin in my arms. It was the nearest thing to actually swimming with killer whales I'd found, and a high point in an ongoing journey that had become both a profound inner experience and an outward happening. I remember the thrill I felt in that moment. I see the absolute joy on my face.

The thrill and the joy I felt were certainly about connecting with that beautiful animal, but they were more—they were about the fact that I *could* connect with that beautiful animal because I'd been able to connect with something beautiful within myself. It was the thrill of victory over fear and the joy of sensing my own potential. René had been right when he said, "Perhaps the part of you that wants to be born has something to do with play, freedom, rest, adventure. I suspect that it will not destroy the world but will be something very creative and positive." Joy with the morning and days of laughter—and a dolphin in my arms. I'm off and running, and I'm not turning back!

I'm Cheering For You!

In his collection of *Good Poems,* Garrison Keillor says, "Stickiness, memorability, is one sign of a good poem. You hear it and a day later some of it is still there in the brainpan."[214] I think it is the sign of a good idea and a good book, too—it sticks because the writer has hit on something true. I hope that as you close the cover of this book, you will find that next week or next year, something of what we've explored together in these pages will have stuck in your mind. It's not important that you remember where you read it or even exactly what it was all about. It does not even matter if it sticks in the conscious part of the brainpan—the unconscious may be better!

If it sticks, I know you'll be able to say a hearty yes to your adventure, the adventure of the hero, of becoming fully human and fully alive. I know you'll be off and running, leaving Egypt, crossing the Red Sea, wandering in the wilderness, and taking your Promised Land. As you run the race of your own transformative journey, imagine me taking a break from my own, cheering you on. You'll hear me calling out, along with everyone in the stands:

"Strength! Courage! Don't be timid; don't get discouraged.
God, your God, is with you every step you take."[215]

"So, boy, don't you turn back.
Don't you set down on the steps
'Cause you finds it's kinder hard.
Don't you fall now—
For I'se still goin', honey,
I'se still climbin'!"

"Don't stop! Further up and further in! Take it in your stride."

---

[214] Garrison Keillor, ed., *Good Poems* (New York, Penguin Books, 2002), p. xix.
[215] Joshua 1:9

And from the Emperor's pavilion, from God himself:

> "Be alert, be present.
> I'm about to do something brand-new. It's bursting out!
> Don't you see it? There it is!"[216]

---

[216] Isaiah 43:18-19

Reflection and Discussion Questions

These questions are intended to stimulate your personal thinking about the ideas and stories in this book. They may be used for small group discussion or for individual reflection.

If for individual reflection, you might want to do some journaling or free writing to jot down your ideas. You might also find someone who would be willing to serve as a safe sounding board for your reactions to the book or to these questions, someone who is able to let you explore without too much personal concern about where your thoughts will lead you. Often, a psychotherapist or pastoral counselor is the ideal companion for your transformative journey.

If for group discussion, you may want to consider adopting the following guidelines. Designed to lead toward deeper levels of personal awareness, these questions ask for a degree of self-disclosure. For this reason, the safety of the group environment cannot be overstressed. I have found that this safety can be enhanced by establishing expectations and ground rules at the outset.

1. Ask for a group commitment to confidentiality: nothing that another person shares will be repeated in any way that might identify him or her.

2. Encourage each member to share only at the level of self-disclosure with which he or she is comfortable.

3. Discourage cross-talk or responses to another's sharing: foster the expectation that each will share their own personal reflections, simply being present and listening to others with no comment, question, insight, or advice. (The last question about the last chapter is an exception to this rule.)

Chapter 1: Transformation, the Hero's Adventure

1. Share what you remember of the Exodus story and where you first remember hearing it.

   What images or moments in the story impressed you or captured your imagination most?

2. What did or do you think of the man Moses?

   Was he someone you think of as a hero?

   What makes someone a hero?

3. What does Joseph Campbell mean when he speaks of "the hero's journey"?[217]

4. Do you identify—right now—with any of the five stages of the transformative journey of the Exodus story?

   Egypt—the Burning Bush or Plagues—the Red Sea—the Wilderness—the Promised Land

---

[217] For further reading on Campbell's ideas, see, for example, *The Hero with a Thousand Faces*.

Chapter 2: The Generations that Come Before

1. Share a little about how you and/or your family came to this country.

   Who were they? Where did they come from? Why did they leave? What happened to them along the way?

   Or, if you don't know these stories, share stories you've heard about your oldest ancestors and/or the oldest member of your family you can personally remember.

   Who were they? What were they like? How did or do you feel about them?

2. What are some characteristics—physical or psychological—or values and philosophies, or valued objects that you have inherited from your family?

3. This chapter explores Joseph's family theme of being chosen or cast out and Susan's family theme of using faith to hold back dangerous human passions. Are there themes—challenges or conflicts—that trace through your family history?

4. What do you think of Robert Johnson's idea that wholeness, not goodness, defines holiness and is God's goal for our lives?

Chapter 3: When Safety Becomes Slavery

1. Share some memories about what gave you a sense of security or safety as a child.

   Was there a special object? A place? A person?

As you grew up, did you outgrow or lose it or them?

If you did, do you remember how it felt? If not, what do you imagine it would be like to give it or them up?

2. What challenges or problems do you remember confronting as a child?

    What did you do to meet or solve them?

    Do you find yourself behaving in similar ways as an adult?

    Are there times these coping strategies don't work for you?

3. What gives you a sense of security or safety now?

    Are there ways in which this has become a burden or is limiting your growth, freedom, or ability to love in some way?

    What fears come up when you think of outgrowing, leaving, or letting go of some aspect of this safety? What longings lie within the choices you have made to find security?

Chapter 4: Where is My Internal Moses?

1. What animal do you think might symbolize your best qualities?

    If you were describing that animal to someone from Mars, what would you say?

    What about that animal particularly appeals to you? List two or three qualities.

Are there ways in which those qualities, at an extreme, might become problematic?

2. Share about a person or group that you really disrespect, reject, cannot stand, or fear. Or, share about something that bothers or concerns you most in your significant other or child.

   If you were describing that person or group to someone from Mars, what would you say?

   What about that person or group particularly bothers you? List two or three characteristics.

3. Since we often project our Shadow onto others, the list you just made of what bothers you about someone else probably indicates something of what you have repressed in yourself. How could this be so? (By the way, the more violently you do *not* believe it could be so is an indication of how deeply you have repressed your Shadow and therefore of how powerfully it will seek recognition. You cannot escape!)

   How might the characteristics you despise or fear be exactly the right balance to the qualities you think best in yourself?

4. This chapter notes that David, Elijah, and Moses all modeled ways of listening within to the still, small voice of God. How do you listen within?

   What appeals to you most when you consider their ways of listening within?

   Might you be willing to commit to listening within in a regular, daily way for the next thirty days?

If so, how, when, and where could you cultivate this practice in your life? Or, if you already have such a daily practice, what might you add or explore to enrich it?

Chapter 5: Homeostasis and Plagues

1. Have you or your family ever had an experience that changed everything ever after?

   What happened? What were your feelings at the time?

2. This chapter proposes the idea that "plagues," often painful and tragic, can be the instrument God uses to disrupt the homeostasis of the systems in which we live, our secure slavery in Egypt. What does that mean about God's stance toward human suffering?

3. What do you make of Sheldon Vanauken's view that his wife's death was a severe mercy?

   What does that phrase, "a severe mercy," mean to you?

   Have you ever had a painful experience that you later came to see as a gift to your life?

   How did this happen?

Chapter 6: The Red Sea

1. Share the story of the most courageous thing you've ever done.

   Bring the scene alive again: consider what you saw, smelled, tasted, heard, felt against your skin or in your body.

What were your feelings, emotional or physical, at the moment of choice?

What choice did you make and what happened as a result?

2. As a rule, how do you tend to make decisions in your life, whether big or little?

What works about your way of deciding and where do you get hung up?

What is the right relationship between feelings, facts or faith, and free will?

3. What in your life requires a courageous choice right now?

What fears would you have to face or what risks would you have to take?

What specific, concrete action would you have to choose in order to move forward?

4. Are you ready to commit, today and to someone else, to take a courageous step forward?

If so, what step and who might be able to support you if they knew?

If not, are you ready to commit to revisit the issue at a specific future date and perhaps with a specific person? Perhaps you might commit to pray about becoming ready to commit or for wisdom to know what would be your courageous choice to move forward.

Chapter 7: Wandering in the Wilderness

1. Can you remember a time when you were forced to wait for something you deeply longed for?

   What happened?

   What did you learn?

2. Check in with the commitment you made to a courageous step forward at the end of the last chapter's reflection questions.

   What progress have you made?

   What have you been feeling, physically or emotionally, as you did or didn't step forward?

   What have you discovered?

3. What do you know about your own speed bump or guardian at the gates of adapting to reality, in other words, your coping or defensive strategies?

   What do you usually do when you feel stressed or anxious?

   When does it work, and when does it not work?

4. Which of the seven lessons of the wilderness do you most need in order to find support for the process your step forward has initiated?

   > Asking for what you need
   > Expecting the unexpected answer
   > Taking it one day at a time

Stop working and rest
Receiving help from others
Holding to the new ways
Remembering who God is

What is one concrete way you will seek to implement that lesson or those lessons this coming week?

Chapter 8: Taking the Promised Land

1. Share a little about your experiences so far in developing a daily practice of listening within, as discussed in chapter four.

2. How do you react to Aphrodite Matsakis' idea that we don't completely eliminate our challenges or the effects of any trauma we may have experienced, but we become "increasingly" better able to confront them and to choose our lives?

3. The Promised Land is about realizing our heart's desires. What is your heart's deepest desire?

   Is there any reality suggesting that you must go deeper to understand your heart's desire? For example, is it possible that the fulfilling of it would hurt another person or would keep you less than you are meant to be? If this is the case, go deeper to the essence of what you long for—then relinquish, not the longing, but the *way* you have been imagining its fulfillment.

   If you had only one prayer request to make for this entire next year, what would it be?

4. How does your transformative journey—the one you are taking as you read this book and work through these reflection questions—support the fulfilling of your heart's desire?

   How is your courageous step forward necessary in moving toward that desire?

   How might a period of waiting be necessary?

   How might the lessons of the wilderness be important when you have attained that desire?

Chapter 9: Scapegoating, Surrender, and Seeds

1. Consider your family when you were a child, perhaps during grade school.

   Who was BIG and who was little in your family?

   Was it okay to be BIG with your parents/caretakers? How did they respond when you felt little?

   What did you learn about being BIG and little from these experiences?

2. Share a memory of a time as a child when you witnessed or experienced a bullying relationship.

   Describe who played each role, BIG and little.

   What were your thoughts and feelings as the bullying went on?

If you could go back to this scene right now, whom would you want to bring with you, and what would you want them to do? How would this change the dynamic between bully and victim, BIG and little?

3. Has there ever been a time, as an adult, when you witnessed or experienced scapegoating?

   Describe the scapegoat. Why do you think they (or you) were chosen?

   Describe the stress or crisis the group was facing when the scapegoating occurred.

   How did the scapegoat behave? How did the group behave?

   What was the outcome?

4. Is there a relationship right now in which you find yourself consistently and inappropriately or exhaustingly in the role of BIG or little, one that doesn't have a good balance and reciprocity between these two elements? Perhaps one you would describe as bullying or scapegoating—or codependent and caretaking?

   What element of Jesus' teaching would you most need to implement in order to change this dynamic?

   > Don't project—see the speck in your own eye

   > Don't identify—you are God's beloved child

   > Do transform by love—pray and forgive

How might you choose to apply that teaching to this situation this week?

Chapter 10: Further Up and Further In!

1. What have you discovered as you have tried to apply Jesus' teaching to that unbalanced relationship you thought about at the end of the last chapter's reflection questions?

   Has anything shifted inside you?

   Has anything shifted in the relationship or has the system resisted change and sought to reestablish homeostasis?

   Is there another element of Jesus' teaching that you would now need to implement to continue supporting the possibility of healthy change in the relationship or in yourself?

2. In which of the five stages of the transformative journey of the Exodus story do you think you are journeying today?

   Has there been any change since you began working through the book and the reflection questions?

3. What do you think about Susan's client's idea that joy comes from recognizing the potential for wholeness that lies within us? This would imply that joy lies more in the exhilaration of the journey and less in an arrival and a finality.

4. What can you celebrate in your own progress on the journey? What can you affirm and celebrate in the others who may have taken this journey with you?

Consider creating a celebration ritual:

> In a group, perhaps you might focus on each member in turn as everyone in the group shares an observation and an affirmation of them.

> As an individual, you might choose to mark your progress with a celebration of some kind: a small purchase, a special meal, a house cleaning, a newly written song or poem, or some other creative effort—a painting, a dance.

Congratulations and bravo for all your hard work in journeying through the book and through these questions. I am cheering for you!

Acknowledgments

What a privilege to acknowledge those who have coached and cheered me along in the process of writing and publishing this book. My mother, Fran Davis, herself a clinical psychologist, has been stalwart in her belief in this work, reading and rereading bits and pieces and whole manuscripts, allowing me to share her deeply personal and often painful story, and grounding me again and again in my faith in the God who is doing a new thing. I am so grateful to her. Other family members have seconded her efforts: my daughters Meagan and Kristen Lansdale, my sister Nancy Davis, my brother Bob Davis, professor of English Literature at Wittenberg College in Springfield, Ohio. I could never have completed this process without their love, thoughtful commentary, and generous willingness to allow me to share the story of our family's journey.

I am so grateful for Eugene Peterson's constant and consistent encouragement that this book was worthy to be shared. He has allowed me to quote liberally from *The Message,* to interrupt him at random intervals with my questions and confusion about the publishing process, and to drop his name shamelessly whenever possible. Even more, he has embraced me as a friend.

My clients have taught me most of what I know and inspired my journey with their own courage and stubborn insistence on life, love, and joy. Each of those whose stories I have shared in these pages unhesitatingly and immediately authorized the telling of their most intimate longings and fears. My students at Fuller Seminary Northern California allowed me to test drive my manuscript with them—required reading for their Pastoral Counseling class last spring—giving me their enthusiastic and energetic feedback. They showed me that even when our theology or traditions may differ, the transformative journey is the hunger of all our hearts.

I have been blessed with some magnificent mentors in my personal and professional journey. My deepest love and profoundest respect is theirs: René Tillich, Michael Horne, Jim Bibb and the psychologists who trained me at The Queen's Medical Center: Carol Nowak, Jean Adair-Leland, and Brian Combs. Thanks to all who took the time to read and offer feedback on the writing and publishing of the book; those as yet unmentioned include Cliff and Joyce Penner, Jeff Kunkel, John Song, Bob Gregg, and Holly Depatie. In addition, I owe a debt of gratitude to Scott Holden, who enthusiastically consulted on title, cover design, and marketing for the book. My heartfelt thanks to all.

About the Author

Susan Davis, Ph.D., is a clinical psychologist in private practice in Redwood City, California, and adjunct assistant professor of pastoral counseling at Fuller Seminary Northern California. The integration of faith and psychological healing has been her passion and focus for the past fifteen years. She also enjoys speaking and leading retreats, and has worked with both Protestant and Catholic churches. You can learn more about her work and contact her through her website: susandavisphd.com.